THE
WITCH'S
CAULDRON

Locally
Crafted
Sage bundles

Laura Tempest Zakroff is a professional artist, author, dancer, designer, muse, mythpunk, teacher, and Witch. She holds a BFA from the Rhode Island School of Design and her artwork has received awards and honors worldwide. Laura has been a practicing Modern Traditional Witch for over two decades and revels in the intersection of her various paths with Witchcraft. She blogs for Patheos as *A Modern Traditional Witch* and for Witches & Pagans as *Fine Art Witchery* and contributes to *The Witches' Almanac*. *The Witch's Cauldron* is her first book, with a second book on sigil witchery due out in 2018. Laura resides in Seattle, Washington, with her partner, Nathaniel Johnstone, and at least three cats. Find out more at www.lauratempestzakroff.com.

THE
WITCH'S
CAULDRON

The Craft, Lore & Magick of Ritual Vessels

LAURA TEMPEST ZAKROFF

Llewellyn Publications
Woodbury, Minnesota

FIRST EDITION
Sixth Printing, 2023

Book series design by Rebecca Zins
Cover design by Shira Atakpu
Cover Illustration by Mickie Mueller
Interior illustrations by Mickie Mueller

Llewellyn Publishing is a registered trademark of

Llewellyn Worldwide Ltd.

Library of Congress Cataloging-in-Publication Data

Names: Tempest Zakroff, Laura, author.

Title: The witch's cauldron : the craft, lore & magick of ritual vessels / Laura Tempest Zakroff.

Description: First Edition. | Woodbury : Llewellyn Worldwide, Ltd., 2017.

Identifiers: LCCN 2017001570 (print) | LCCN 2017011790 (ebook) | ISBN 9780738752525 (ebook) | ISBN 9780738750392

Subjects: LCSH: Witchcraft. | Magic.

Classification: LCC BF1566 (ebook) | LCC BF1566 .T37 2017 (print) | DDC 133.4/3--dc23

LC record available at https://lccn.loc.gov/2017001570

Llewellyn Publications
A Division of Llewellyn Worldwide Ltd.
2143 Wooddale Drive
Woodbury, MN 55125-2989
www.llewellyn.com
Printed in the United States of America

Other Works by Laura Tempest Zakroff

Coloring Books

Steampunk Menagerie

(2015)

Myth & Magick

(2016)

The Art of Bellydance

(2016)

Witch's Brew

(2016)

Instructional DVDs

Bellydance Artistry

(2011)

DecoDance

(2015)

Contributions

Witches & Pagans and *SageWoman* magazines
(Illustrator, BBI Media)

The Witches' Almanac, Spring 2017–2018, 2018–2019
(Contributing author, The Witches' Almanac, LTD)

The Witch's Book of Shadows by Jason Mankey
(Contributing author, Llewellyn, 2017)

IN LOVING *memory of my grandfather Marty, who instilled a sense of magic, art, and natural wonder in my life, and my grandmother Natalie, who stirred, brewed, and crafted many delicious meals from a big pot in a tiny kitchen.*

contents

The Modern Traditional Witch Perspective

You may find some of the opinions and approaches to certain practices in this book a little out of the ordinary. I am a Modern Traditional Witch—a path that blends the folklore, myths, and practices of my complex and diverse heritage with the acknowledgment that I am a modern person living in the United States. I have studied a multitude of paths, mostly from an academic standpoint, but have found that a blend of old-world and new-world witchery is the best personal approach for me. That means sometimes an old practice can find new meaning with new information, tools, and interpretation. "Because that's the way it always has been done" is not an acceptable mode of thinking, especially if our ancestors made use of technology as it advanced through the centuries. A good example would be the option of rubbing sticks together versus using matches or a lighter to make fire. It's definitely good to know how to do it the old way, but it's just as effective and more efficient to make use of the new way.

The tenants of my tradition are made up of three keys of practice:

Know Thyself: This concept means to be aware of your strengths and weaknesses—mentally, spiritually, and physically.

Maintain Balance: This point is not just about focusing on moderation, but also about understanding extremes and working with them. It also means understanding that every action and intention has possible positive and negative effects. Whether something is positive or negative (helpful or harmful) has a lot to do with perspective.

Accept Responsibility: The last key is being able to acknowledge, accept, and work with both the known and unknown consequences of your actions and words.

What does that all mean? I take into consideration what the outcome of any working might be, beyond my own intention. I try to be mindful of my own limitations as well as those of others. I offer what I believe can be helpful instead of hurtful. I do like my poetry, ritual, and mystical art, but I also make significant use of common sense, modern conveniences, and especially humor. I long ago discovered that the spirits and deities I work with are not without their own sense of humor, so while I take my work seriously, I have learned not to get too bogged down with my actual practice. I have found that being lighthearted while also grounded makes for powerful, effective magick. It also makes life much more interesting, in the best of ways.

It's important to keep in mind that there is never just one way to do something. Allow yourself to be creative! I encourage you to use this book to expand your own practice while also having some fun in the process. Blessings!

Introduction

Few symbols are as commonly linked with Witchcraft as the cauldron. From Ceridwen to the weyward Sisters in Shakespeare's *Macbeth*, when it comes to conjuring, the cauldron has played an iconic role in portraying the Witch's power in our collective consciousness for hundreds—if not thousands—of years. So many myths and stories from around the world center on the Witch and her cauldron.

It's easy to imagine a darkened room, lit only by a hearth fire, upon which a cauldron bubbles, steam pouring forth from a mystical brew; or the classic picture of a cauldron sitting upon a tripod in the center of a magick circle, surrounded by a group of Witches who chant while tossing in herbs and other mysterious ingredients. The wonder and mystery of the cauldron is that it truly is, at its heart, a simple yet very functional household item. That may seem strange to many of us today, with our microwaves and fancy cookware, but for many people around the world, the cauldron was at the center of cooking, cleaning, and other utilitarian tasks.

The weyward Sisters, hand in hand

The true power of the Witch is her ability to transform an ordinary vessel into a means of making magick, right before our eyes. In dangerous times, it was safer to have a commonplace item that could double for a person's spiritual needs while not outing them to those who might wish to cause them harm. It was also the best way to stretch a limited budget or lack of space. So just as the broom could both clean the floor and be used for "flight," the cauldron could not only cook dinner but also be enlisted to make magical potions, be the center of a ritual, talk to the gods, and divine the future.

Nowadays, most modern Witches don't have to worry about being persecuted for their ways, and we also tend to like collecting tools and objects of the trade that please us. It's important to uncover the meaning behind those tools in order to use them to the best of our abilities and fully enjoy them. In this book, we will explore the history of the cauldron as well as the mythology around it. I will provide a wide variety of options for you to consider when selecting your own cauldron (or cauldrons!), from making your own, to purchasing a new one, to thrifting and upcycling other items to be used instead. We will explore how to use a cauldron, including blessing it, using it in ritual, working spellcraft with it, practicing kitchen witchery, divining the future, and taking good care of it. I will also pull in some old-world witchery and apply it in new ways to some undercover and unconventional cauldrons that are probably already in your home. You'll see that the possibilities for this wonderful tool are endless, and it may just become your favorite!

chapter
1

Meet the Cauldron

The Cauldron is steeped in folklore and has been represented in art for centuries, yet at the same time is a humble and ubiquitous object. It is at the center of mythic magical workings and supernatural transformations *and* is also used to make dinner and clean up. Probably no other tool quite embodies the essence of the modern-day Witch, who every day is faced with balancing the mystical with the mundane, just like the cauldron does.

Defining the Cauldron

When you hear or see the word *cauldron*, you most likely think instantly of the classic image of a cauldron: a curvaceous, wide-bellied black pot with a slightly narrower lipped opening, probably with handles, a trio of legs, and a lid. And there's a good reason for that: the design of the cauldron has remained essentially unchanged for centuries. To see why, let's look first at some definitions and possible origins of this vessel.

cauldron =

"a large pot used for boiling, especially one with handles" [from earlier *cauderon*, from Anglo-French, from Latin *caldārium* hot bath, from *calidus* warm]
—*Collins English Dictionary*

"a large kettle or boiler" [Middle English *cauderon* <Anglo French < Late Latin *caldāria*, n. use of feminine of Latin *caldārius* of warming, derivative of *calidus* warm, *calēre* to be warm]
—*Random House Kernerman Webster's College Dictionary*

As the root words suggest, the typical cauldron was designed especially for heating and boiling liquids. The rounded shape allows for easy stirring and provides more surface area, increasing evaporation (ideal for making stews and similar reductions) and helping to prevent boiling over. (If you've ever had your pasta water boil over on your stove, imagine trying to stop the same thing from happening in a large, heavy suspended pot!) No matter where you look around the world, you'll find that every culture developed a similarly shaped pot as a solution to heating liquids.

A collection of cauldrons

Cauldron Basics

The cauldron is first and foremost a container. It is shaped to hold things and is designed to conduct and retain heat. Cauldrons are most commonly made of metal, usually iron, for extra durability and longevity. For ease of handling, a cauldron typically has at least two handles, which can be used for carrying, pouring, and suspension by hook and chain. The vessel may be slightly flattened on the bottom so it will rest on a surface, or more commonly set with three legs that form a tripod so it may sit above a fire. Lastly, the cauldron is finished off with a fitted lid, which helps to contain whatever is being brewed inside it. Since the shape of a cauldron makes liquid evaporate more quickly, a lid comes in handy to slow down that process, collect condensation, and maintain warmth after cooking.

Typically, cauldrons were of a significant size so that a meal for a family or household could be prepared within it and washing could also be done. Meals and beverages would be portioned out to smaller containers (bowls, cups, and plates). It is important to note that the mammoth-size cauldrons you see in many artistic works depicting Witches from the late Middle Ages onward definitely reflect some significant artistic license. Very large cauldrons would have been extremely expensive to obtain, not to mention rather difficult to drag out into the middle of the woods. On the opposite end of the size spectrum, the tiny cauldrons sold in metaphysical and occult shops today are made with modern practitioners in mind, who are using other vessels to cook their food and do their wash. Some brilliant person figured out that we love to buy miniature things, practical or not!

Unpacking Symbolism

It's easy to assign a variety of symbolic meanings to the cauldron, with its classic size, shape, and uses. But how many of those meanings make sense today? Let's reexamine the cauldron symbolism that has been handed down over the last several decades and look at it with a fresh eye.

Within modern Pagan paths, the cauldron is most commonly equated with the womb, making it inherently "female" by relation and associated with goddesses. It's important to remember that most household chores (cooking, washing, etc.) were often considered to be the domain of women. It's this connection to womanly duties that linked Witches and cauldrons together in our collective consciousness, as the Witch hunts were rooted in social and gender politics, despite the veil of religious propaganda. Or we could link the cauldron to the womb, with the understanding that if we put the right ingredients in it, something will be born out of it—but that does seem rather crass when simplified like that. I don't think that comparison is fair to the womb bearers *or* the cauldrons.

I've seen multiple sources claim that the tripod of legs on a cauldron is meant to symbolize the triple goddess. This idea is charming, but the design fairy in me must point out that a tripod of legs is ideal for setting down a cauldron on possibly uneven ground. One or two legs is simply not functional, as it would make for easy tipping and spillage, and four legs works only if both the surface is flat and the legs are perfectly even. Hence, three legs makes for the most efficient design. But if it gives you warm fuzzies to associate the triple legs with a deity concept, by all means go for it. Symbols *are* about the power of connection, relating the physical to the metaphysical.

It is my belief that viewing the cauldron as female in modern Pagan practice is more strongly linked with the desire to revive the concept of the Goddess than with the cauldron's shape or use. In the mid- to late twentieth century, there was much emphasis put on connecting Neopagan practices to the Old Religion and fighting patriarchal concepts with matriarchal ones or more balanced ideas. When we consider the countercultures of post–World War II society, this makes a great deal of sense. There was a lot of energy put into aligning the practice with binary genders—cups and cauldrons as tools of the Goddess and thus feminine, and wands and athames as masculine, used in turn by priest and priestess. Applying gendered symbolism can certainly help some people feel more connected to an item and connect with a possibly forgotten past, but it can also alienate some—especially those outside of the gender binary. There's a lot more to the cauldron than anatomical references, and it should be a comfortable tool for anyone to use.

As we will see in chapter 2, the cauldron is not inherently female or strictly Goddess-oriented. What brings us the most profound symbolism of the cauldron is not its shape, but how it has played a role in practices and myths for centuries. I hope you will find inspiration in the meaning that you can derive from the myths, stories, and folklore. In the end, the symbolism that is most important is that which is validated by *your* experience and *your* practice. If an idea inspires you and feels right, then you're on the right track!

The Nine Uses of the Cauldron

To get us in the proper frame of mind, I have devised a system to help describe the uses and applications of cauldrons. This system consists of nine categories inspired by the roles and purposes of cauldrons in myth, folklore, history, and ritual. This list will help you determine how to use your own cauldron and enable you to find personal meaning and purpose in related activities. It is quite possible that you will find overlap between categories, which is perfectly natural since the cauldron is so multifunctional.

The Container: In its simplest function, the cauldron is a holder. In this form, it's relatively passive—whatever it contains is in its final form already, and the cauldron protects and preserves it. Examples of this would be when the cauldron is used to hold wine before it's distributed or hold written intentions collected for a ritual. It can also symbolize a repository of the owner's power.

The Maker: Unlike the container mode, the maker is active. This state is when the cauldron is being used to brew, prepare, cook, or dye. It is an agent in physically changing the properties of the ingredients mixed within it. Examples would be brewing mead, cooking a stew, or dyeing cloth.

The Transformer: Akin to the maker, the transformer goes beyond physical changes into metaphysical changes, such as charging a pendant, burning an intention, releasing a binding, or making an offering. The cauldron can act as a crucible—physically, as in metalmaking, when molten metal is poured into a mold, or metaphorically, such as during the casting of a spell.

The Purifier: This state is for cleaning, cleansing, and renewal —from boiling water in a cauldron to make it safe to drink, to washing items or making a cleansing bath.

The Gateway: In some traditions, the cauldron hung from a chain in a hearth or from a tripod symbolizes the connection between this realm and the divine. The chain becomes a kind of telephone line, making the cauldron a gateway to the gods. Sometimes the cauldron is a literal passage to another realm or dimension (such as the Underworld). When the cauldron is used as a means of transportation, it falls in the gateway category.

The Marker: The marker is the mode in which the cauldron is used ritually as a placeholder or guide. It can be a type of altar, the center of a ritual working, or help define sacred space. As a marker, the cauldron can act as a type of spiritual homing beacon for the Witch who may be spiritually (or physically) traveling on a vision flight or riding to the sabbat.

The Drum: In traditions that are rooted in nomadic paths, the cauldron has multiple duties, including transforming into a percussive instrument—such as a drum or a kind of bell. Musical applications may be for spiritual purposes or for entertainment and merrymaking. Metaphorically, the cauldron can also represent the heartbeat of a group, tribe, or coven—something that pulls them all together and unifies them, especially through a communal meal or shared beverage.

Divination: There are multiple ways that a cauldron can be used in divining the present, past, or future, such as scrying, lot casting, pyromancy (divination by fire), libanomancy (smoke/incense), carromancy (melting wax), ceromancy (dripping wax on water), eleomancy (oil), or hydromancy (water).

Rebirth: The cauldron as a state of rebirth has elements of the other conditions, such as the transformer, the gateway, and the purifier, but its power to give or renew life itself sets it apart because of the magnitude of its power. It is in this state that the cauldron most closely embodies the womb, as it gives new life.

As we dive into the history and myth of the cauldron, consider the roles the cauldron plays, and think about which of the nine uses each role falls in. This will give you insight and inspiration into how you can best use your own cauldron.

Word Play

I've always found it fascinating how words originate, travel, and morph over time. Here are some variations for *kettle* and *cauldron* in other languages:

Kettle: German: *kessel*; Middle English: *chetel*; Old Norse: *ketill*

Cauldron: Middle Irish: *coiri* or *caere;* Welsh: *pair* or *peir*

It's especially interesting how variations become incorporated into new words and ideas. Take, for instance, *caldera*. A *caldera* is a circular depression or similar formation in the earth, caused by volcanic activity (and is sometimes called a cauldron).

A variation can even become a proper name! Take, for instance, *kazan*, which is the Turkish word for cauldron, and *kazanci*, which is a cauldron worker. Kazan is also a common last name now in both Turkey and Greece. In Greece, it's the shortened form of *Kazandzis*, a vocational description for a maker of cauldrons or one who uses a cauldron for the distillation of spirits.

Gather Round—The Cauldron in History & Myth

The cauldron! How it ignites our imagination! For centuries we have gathered around the cauldron in its hearth, cooked our meals, celebrated our harvests, brewed our drinks, washed ourselves, and told our stories and myths. The cauldron has had many roles, from practical to metaphysical. To get to know this vessel more intimately, we'll look at its development in history and then explore its deep involvement in many a cultural myth.

> *Double, double toil and trouble;*
> *Fire burn, and cauldron bubble*
> —William Shakespeare's *Macbeth*

The Hidden Cauldron

When looking for historic examples of cauldrons, you'll be very hard-pressed to find complete surviving examples. The reason is largely because the cauldron was such an all-purpose tool. It was employed until it didn't work anymore, and then it was either destroyed or recycled. Unless a vessel had very special spiritual purpose or stature, it was used only for as long as it functioned. Sadly, if the background of those spiritual purposes did not align with a conquering culture, the vessel was most likely melted down and made into something else. The few surviving examples of cauldrons that we do have tend to be more elaborate, specialized vessels that were discovered at burial sites.

Another factor that impedes investigation and exploration of the comprehensive history of the cauldron is that it became relegated to the realm of household duties, particularly that of the feminine persuasion. Women's work has typically drawn less serious attention from the largely male-dominated fields of history, archaeology, and anthropology over the previous centuries than items considered to be of the masculine domain, such as weaponry and armor, farming tools, etc. This unbalanced view further emphasizes why the tools most associated with Witches (cauldrons, brooms) and, of course, commonly used by women make appearances in the Witch-hunting lore. It was common for Witch hunters to pervert simple, available tools to fit their claims, just as any typical birthmark could be used to prove someone was a Witch, and the accusations fueled the imagination of artists. But during that era, a cauldron was just a tool, owned by any person who could afford to purchase one or had the skill to make one. Basically, it was the equivalent of the microwave of today. As more and more interest is invested in discovering how our female ancestors lived and worked, we may discover new and interesting information about the history of the cauldron.

The History and Development of the Cauldron

Every human civilization has developed a type of cauldron, primarily in order to satisfy the need to carry and transport fire and water. As a species early on, we discovered the many benefits of fire: for warmth, as a tool for building and hunting, and, of great importance to the history of the cauldron, for cooking. Cooking our food allowed us to spend less time chewing and processing it and to preserve it longer, which helped to develop and enlarge our brains as we evolved. Cooking also likely led to the happy accident of discovering the benefits of purifying water by boiling it—that is, as long as you had something to put it in!

At first, we crafted our vessels from natural resources. Mollusks, turtle shells, skullcaps, animal bladders, gourds, and coconuts all were utilized to contain and cook. As we learned how to use fire to transform clay and to work malleable metals, we experimented to find the best way to build a durable, lasting container that could hold liquid and also be used to prepare food—first in copper, then in bronze, and then, starting about two thousand years ago, in cast iron.

The needs of a civilization influenced the evolution of the vessel and its usage within it. Those of a primarily nomadic lifestyle required more of an all-in-one vessel to ease the weight they carried with them. Consider the Sahrawi people of the western Sahara in North Africa, one of the many nomadic Berber tribes. In addition to cooking, their vessel has been used for centuries to carry fire and water and, when fitted with a skin, as a drum for celebration and ritual. That's efficiency! I would like to point out that just because they use one primary vessel for many tasks does not mean they are primitive by any means. The Berber people are known to be highly skilled in metalwork, textiles, and other greatly valued goods. When trade is your main source of income, it's vitally important to have more room for your stock than, say, a drum, cooking pots, fire pots, etc.

Nomadic life

People who focused on building settlements centered on farming and animal husbandry eventually developed indoor hearth technology. The indoor fireplace in turn led to further advancements in the variety of cookware—as well as the mythology surrounding these vessels. Ritual, practice, and social protocol for the cauldron developed as the culture did. As we track the Bronze and Iron Ages across the globe, especially throughout the Asian and European continents, we start to find surviving artifacts of cauldrons and their related accessories.

Fabulous Feasting Cauldrons from History

The British Museum has several wonderful ancient cauldron artifacts in its collection. There's the Battersea Cauldron (estimated to be from 800–600 BCE, late Bronze Age into Early Iron Age). It's a fairly large cauldron, constructed from seven sheets of bronze, painstakingly shaped, curved, and riveted together. Such an investment of time and resources suggests that this cauldron (and ones like it) would have been highly treasured and most likely used for a chieftain's feasts. Also in the British Museum collection, there is a smaller cauldron than the Battersea, likewise made of bronze (and estimated to be from 1–50 CE). Its construction is similar: bronze sheet held together by rivets that have large decorative heads, and its mouth was most likely made by rolling the flat bronze sheeting around an iron ring. Since it's significantly smaller than the Battersea, it's considered an especially rare find, since it could cook much less food and was not ideal for a large feasting celebration or ownership by a chief. I would hazard to guess that its survival is due to it being a very special cauldron to someone of a different stature—perhaps the tribal healer—and it was buried with that person as a favored or sacred object, ensuring its survival until its discovery.

The Battersea Cauldron

Interesting cauldron accessories that you can also find at the British Museum are what have been classified as "flesh hooks" from the Bronze and Iron Ages. It is suggested that these artifacts may have been used to scoop meat from the cauldron while feasting. Some of them are very detailed and elaborate, suggesting special or ritual purposes. One such example is the Bronze Age flesh hook that was found in a bog at Dunaverney in 1829 and was recently radiocarbon-dated to 1050 and 900 BCE. It has a patterned wooden section decorated with studded bronze pieces, as well as a pair of birds that look to be ravens, and five waterfowl appearing to be two swans and their three cygnets—or perhaps ducks.

At the Ashmolean Museum at the University of Oxford, you can see another example of a large Bronze Age cauldron that was uncovered by bathers in 1928 in the bed of the River Cherwell at Shipton-on-Cherwell, Oxfordshire. It's dated to be from 1100–1000 BCE and is classified as an "Atlantic cauldron," which refers to cauldrons found in areas of Europe touched by the Atlantic Ocean, including Britain, Ireland, France, and the Iberian Peninsula. This cauldron is made of three sheets of bronze: two rectangular pieces that create the circumference of the body, and a circular bowl-shaped piece joined on the bottom. It also features two cast handles at its neck for carrying or suspending. The body shows a long history of repairs, suggesting that it was kept in use for feasts and treasured for a long time before it ended up in the river.

In 2004, a cache of twelve large cauldrons was discovered at a site near the village of Chiseldon, North Wiltshire, in the United Kingdom—the largest group of Iron Age cauldrons ever to be discovered in Europe that we have on historical record. They were buried together with two cow skulls, as well as evidence of pottery and other vessels that date to 800–100 BCE. The cauldrons had been stacked or placed in the ground, with about half of them positioned upside down, and the rest were either on their side or mouth up. They range from between twenty-four to thirty-two inches wide at the rim and are made of a mixture of copper alloy and iron. To allow for intact research, the site was lifted complete in soil blocks and transported for study by the British Museum. The cauldrons are still being explored today, and you can follow the progress at blog.britishmuseum.org, under the "Chiseldon cauldrons" tag.

There are more examples of cauldrons to be found in the dark corners of many a museum, especially in Europe. While the feasting cauldrons definitely have significant importance to historians and archaeologists, they're not as visually exciting to the general public or as sexy to study as weaponry, jewelry, and other crafts from that era. Unless, of course, they're quite spectacular, like our next famous cauldron…

Sacrificial and Sacred Cauldrons

If you visit the National Museum of Denmark in Copenhagen, you can feast your eyes on the original Gundestrup Cauldron (there are life-size replicas at several other European museums). It is estimated to have been made in the second or first century BCE and was found in a peat bog in Gundestrup, Denmark, in 1891. Most people are surprised to learn that it was not found intact, but rather was discovered in pieces and reconstructed for display. A fabulously decorated cauldron made of silver, it is the largest known example of European Iron Age, measuring twenty-seven inches in diameter and seventeen inches high. The decoration was made by carefully hammering the silver sheeting from the reverse side to create a raised design, in addition to gold gilding and glass inlay. Despite it being discovered in Denmark, there are theories that it may be Gaulish or Thracian in origin, due to the craftsmanship and imagery.

It is the imagery in particular that has led to photos and drawings of the Gundestrup Cauldron appearing in many a Pagan book that touches upon history and roots. The base plate of the cauldron depicts a sword-wielding female figure and two dogs surrounding a bull, engaged in combat. The seven exterior plates each have a central bust or portrait—four bearded male figures and three female, each with a distinct scene and additional people and animals, including a boar, a winged horse, a dragon, a stag, birds of prey, and a lion. All are wondrously detailed, yet the interior plates are what steal the show. The one you may be most familiar with is the portrait of Cernunnos. This plate shows a seated man with antlers holding a torc in his right hand and a horned serpent in the left, surrounded by a similarly antlered stag and an array of other animals and plant designs. The other interior plates include a portrait of a woman wearing a torc next to pairs of six-spoked wheels, elephants, and griffins; a bull-slaying scene repeated over three times; and what appears to be warriors marching, being dipped into a cauldron and then reborn to march out again. Keep in mind this last scene when we explore cauldron mythology!

Cernunnos on the Gundestrup Cauldron

Gather Round—
The Cauldron in History & Myth

It's interesting to note that the discovery of the Gundestrup Cauldron spawned several imitations—cauldron conspiracies, if you will! The most famous of these is the Chiemsee Cauldron, found at the bottom of Lake Chiemsee in Bavaria in 2001. Made of eighteen-carat gold and weighing over twenty-three pounds, it is decorated in a Celtic style very similar to the Gundestrup. After scientific examination and subsequent sleuthing, it was found to be a twentieth-century creation made by Otto Gahr (with the help of Munich goldsmith Alfred Notz), a silversmith and Nazi Party member, for Albert Pietzsch, who was a wealthy man and Nazi Party supporter. My research also uncovered references to an Italian-based forgery from the 1920s and other "inspired" pieces, but very little information about them. I suppose all parties involved in those discoveries would have been rather embarrassed.

The Gundestrup is often described as a "sacrificial cauldron," as its elaborate facade and silverwork suggest that it wasn't your typical feasting cauldron. When we hear the word *sacrificial*, the more macabre corners of our minds tend to picture a cauldron upon which blood is poured or spilled. This line of thinking is heavily influenced by certain myths in which the gods or heroes are reduced to a pile of bones and reborn in the cauldron, or perhaps by the stories (often told by the Christian Romans) of the Pagans of olden days making human sacrifices to ensure the fertility of the crops and the animals. But the archaeological evidence we see of actual sacrificial "cauldrons" tends to refer to the creation of elaborate works of art that were purposely dismembered and buried—possibly as offerings to the gods or to the land. Or maybe the Gundestrup Cauldron wasn't dismembered purposely for the gods, but was destroyed and disposed of by conquering forces offended by the imagery upon it—though one would think they would have melted it down for the silver, which is possibly the unfortunate fate of many a sacred cauldron.

This brings us to the cauldrons of Dodona in Greece. You may have heard of the Oracle of Delphi, but do you know about the Oracle of Dodona, considered to be the oldest in Greece? The legend, according to Herodotus, says that it was founded by one of two black doves that flew from Thebes in Egypt and landed in an oak tree at Dodona, announcing that a sanctuary to Zeus was to be built there. (The other dove landed in Libya and made a similar proclamation.) The doves of the story are thought to be a metaphor for a pair of dark-skinned priestesses from an oracular tradition who escaped from Egypt and settled in Greece, and not actual birds—though the connection to the oak tree is rather nice. The legend goes on to say that from the eighth to the fourth centuries BCE, a number of bronze cauldrons on tripods were carefully arranged around the oak tree, touching each other—and causing them all to sound when one was struck. The chiming and tones of the cauldrons, as well as the wind upon the rustling oak leaves, were interpreted by the priestesses as divine answers. Several other accounts make note of a bronze statue of a boy holding a whip that had three flexible chains suspended from it—and it's suggested that it was this whip that was used to strike the cauldrons and call upon the voice of Zeus.

Many famous heroes from Greek mythology made a stop in Dodona and consulted the Oracle, including Jason of the Argonauts, Odysseus, and Achilles, as well as kings and rulers from the historical record. The oak tree that grows there now is a modern replacement, but bronze fragments of tripods and cauldrons dating back to the era of the Oracle have been found there. It is speculated that the Oracle at Dodona was destroyed by invading forces and the cauldrons and tripods melted down for weaponry.

Our next cauldron in this category is one of ancient history that has been revived by modern practice: the Cauldron of the Olympic Flame. Also related to Zeus in a way, it commemorates Prometheus stealing fire from Zeus and gifting it to humanity. It is said to have been kept burning throughout the duration of the original ancient Olympics. The Olympic Cauldron found its way back into the modern Olympic Games in the summer of 1928 in Amsterdam, and has been a tradition ever since.

The flame is kindled for the Games in Olympia, Greece, at the Temple of Hera. There, eleven woman representing Vestal Virgins perform a rite in which the rays of the sun are concentrated by a parabolic mirror, starting the fire. The lighted torch first travels around Greece and then is transferred to the host city. For every occasion of the Olympic Games, a new cauldron, pedestal, and torch are designed—and at least these modern sacred cauldrons are revered and cherished by their host cities.

The Cauldron Game

Considering the theme of the Olympic Games, sports, and conquests, we might stop and consider the resemblance of many trophies to cauldrons. Particularly in the nineteenth and twentieth centuries, we can see examples of many oversized cups suitable for feasting or a large group of people to drink out of. A prominent example that springs to mind is the National Hockey League's Stanley Cup, which started life as a decorative silver punch bowl and was first presented in 1893. In 1896, the Winnipeg Victorias started the tradition of the team drinking champagne from the Cup after winning it—a lovely example of community feasting and celebration. The winning and display of the Cup is a great honor and a source of pride for the team and its city—not unlike those tribal feasting cauldrons of old.

Keep all these historical cauldrons in mind as you read the next section, where we explore the various roles the cauldron has played in mythology.

The Mythic Cauldron

While historic artifacts are indeed quite rare, the cauldron itself is an integral part of many a myth in numerous cultures. The nature of myth is that as it travels from culture to culture, the names and details of key players shift, change, or are obliterated, so it's impossible to cover them all in one neat, tidy book. With that in mind, I have selected some of the most prominent, pervasive, and topically relevant myths to explore here. We'll look at the stories themselves and the symbolism behind them, and consider what truths the myths may hold for us.

The Cauldron and the Divine Feminine

In this section, we'll take a close look at the connection of the cauldron with women and goddesses from myth and legend. One theme in all of these myths is that the cauldron symbolizes the power of the subject to conduct magick. Its presence is testament to a woman's power to work potions, unseen spirits, and the elements—to work outside of the natural order of things.

Ceridwen's Cauldron

The Celtic realm is bursting with cauldron mythos, one of the most notable being that of Ceridwen and her cauldron. Ceridwen is considered by those who follow modern Celtic Pagan paths to be a goddess of transformation, rebirth, and creative inspiration. Her story comes to us from medieval Welsh legends ("The Tale of Taliesin" from *The Mabinogion*) and speaks of her skill as an accomplished sorceress and how she came to give birth to a legendary bard.

The Story: Ceridwen had two children, a beautiful and blessed daughter named Creirwy and a hideously ugly son named Afagddu. In order to help out her son, Ceridwen decided to make a special potion in her cauldron (which was called Awen) that would grant him incredible wisdom and poetic inspiration. The brew had to be boiled for a year and a day to come to fruition, so she had a blind man named Morda tend to the fire and a dopey village boy named Gwion Bach stir it. Imagine conducting a spell so important to you that you designate your cauldron for this one specific use for an entire year!

According to the spell, the first three drops from the potion would create the desired effect, but the rest would be worthless and full of poison. As it so happened, upon the final day of brewing, three hot drops splashed out of the cauldron and landed on the hand of young Gwion, burning him. He instinctively put his hand to his mouth to soothe the burn, thereby taking in the wisdom that had been intended for Ceridwen's son. With his newfound knowledge, Gwion understood that Ceridwen would be furious, and fled.

Upon discovering that her carefully prepared potion had been spoiled and that Gwion was gone, Ceridwen knew what had happened and set after him, beginning an epic chase. Gwion turned himself into a hare, and she a greyhound. He jumped into a river and became a salmon, and she became an otter. He turned into a songbird, and she a hawk. He became a single grain within a large pile, and she turned into a hen and then found him and ate him.

Yet somehow, perhaps due to the power of the potion, Gwion was not destroyed, and in defiance of biology, Ceridwen became pregnant with him. She resolved to kill him when he was born, but found herself unable to do so. Instead she put him in a container and tossed him into the ocean, where he was rescued by a prince and grew up to become the legendary bard, poet, and magician Taliesin.

The Symbolism: Many folks see the cauldron as representing the womb, especially in connection with Ceridwen, but if we give a critical eye to this story, we see that the cauldron is used to try to accomplish what her own womb could not: to make her son great. Ceridwen is the classic mother, wanting to do what's best for her child, and she is understandably angry when her plans go awry. And yet it's through her own body (and womb) that Gwion is able to become Taliesin. The transformation doesn't happen *in* the cauldron, but through the brew that was mixed within it. The key role of the cauldron is that it is a powerful tool at the disposal of a practiced magick worker, and it acts as maker, container, and transformer. Through it, the potion is made and held and becomes the source of change and transformation.

Cauldron Consideration: Even with the best of intentions, planning, tools, and power, you can't always control the outcome, and some things cannot be changed, no matter how hard you try. Sometimes it's best to let inspiration manifest on its own terms.

Stirring the Cauldron: The Cauldron of Inspiration

THERE IS PERHAPS no greater symbol of magick and the workings of magick than the Witch's cauldron. Picture it if you will. It is deep and round. There is a powerful concoction of herbs and flowers and potent intentions simmering away inside of it. The elixir, once distilled, contains the properties to bring the dead back to life or to grant unimagined inspiration to the one who but tastes of it. And of all those cauldrons, there is one like no other: the Cauldron of Ceridwen.

Ceridwen, as recounted in the *Chronicle of Six Ages of the World* by Elis Gruffudd and by storytellers before and since, decides to brew a potion like no other. To do this, she must gather the ingredients for a year and a day and add them to her cauldron in just the right amounts on just the right days. The resulting extract will bestow upon Afagddu, her most unfortunate son, the powers of knowledge and wisdom.

The nature of such a spell requires that the cauldron boil continuously and be stirred repeatedly throughout the duration of the working. To ensure this happens, Ceridwen enlists the help of Morda, the stoker, and Gwion Bach, the stirrer. As this transpires, the cauldron has other ideas about who should receive such an awe-inspiring draught, and Ceridwen's plans take quite an unexpected turn. As the story goes, once the three Awen-filled drops of liquid pass the lips of the recipient, the cauldron breaks in two and the potion becomes poison. But is such a cauldron meant for just one spell? The answer is not hard. The answer is yes and no.

The cauldron is the container of the magick, and without it the potion could not be steeped. Its cast-iron walls become imbued with Ceridwen's intentions, or perhaps those intentions resided in the very atoms of the cauldron all along. In this way, the cauldron and the compound properties it contains *are* meant for just one purpose, one use, one person. However, this is no ordinary cauldron, for it holds the mysteries of the universe within it. *That* version of the cauldron is not limited to a single ferrous form, but rather appears when needed, when the time is right, and when wisdom and knowledge and inspiration and magick are called for in the world.

It is this cauldron that Ceridwen uses to create her magick. It is to this cauldron that Witches throughout time have added their own herbs. It is from this cauldron that Witches still draw their magick today. And, as it always has been and always will be, this Cauldron of Inspiration is the underlying agency that supports the profound work of transformation and magick.

Gwion Raven
Priestess, Witch & teacher •
www.tobeawitch.com

Baba Yaga's Flying Cauldron

Near and dear to my heart is Baba Yaga, the classic Witch crone of Slavic and Russian folklore.

The Story: Baba Yaga makes numerous appearances in the fairy tales and folklore of Eastern Europe and what's been known historically (and in some parts, currently) as Russia.

She is said to be an old woman of considerable age, at times looking like a dear grandmother and at others like a hideous balding monster with an oversized nose and iron teeth. Similarly, she is known for being both malevolent and benevolent, which depends mainly on her mood and what she thinks she can get from you.

Baba Yaga has been said to fly around in a large cauldron—or an oversized mortar and pestle—stirring it to make it move or using it as a rudder. This peculiarity can be seen as a distorted sexual reference, but whether her flying vehicle of choice is a cauldron or a mortar, they are both indicative of tools of her trade as a Witch. The stories also make mention of her holding a silver birch broom to sweep away any trace of her as she moves about—another interesting Witch tool reference! She resides deep in the forest in a bewitched hut that stands on one or more chicken legs—so it too can also move about. When it's stationary, it's surrounded by an imposing fence made of human bones, ablaze with burning skulls—such haute macabre style!

Symbolism: Baba Yaga represents everything that cannot be controlled. She is death, she is the Spirit of the Forest, she is the woman over whom no man has any power. You never know if she will help you or harm you. Her cauldron is a symbol of her trade as a powerful Witch and acts as a gateway by transporting her to where she wants to be.

Baba Yaga flying

Cauldron Consideration: Nature is about balance and mystery. It can both aid and destroy us, give us comfort or scare us. Magick can both harm and heal as well; it's all about your will. Exercise caution and treat both nature and magick with respect.

Circe's Brew

Circe is a goddess/enchantress in Greek mythology said to be the daughter of the Titan Helios and the Oceanid Perse. Her brother was Aeetes, keeper of the Golden Fleece, and her sister was Pasiphaë, the wife of King Minos and mother of the Minotaur—so Circe was part of a family at the root of magical happenings in Greece! Her particular power is related to her potions as well as her knowledge of necromancy.

The Story: Circe makes a prominent appearance in Homer's *Odyssey.* During their adventures, Odysseus and his crew reach Colchys, the island where Circe lives in a grand palace, surrounded by fierce-looking animals (wolves, lions, boars) that all seem amazingly docile. She invites them to attend a feast, which everyone but Odysseus goes to, and nearly all of them drink of her enchanted potion—turning them into pigs. One man escapes to tell the tale to Odysseus.

The god Hermes (via Athena) provides Odysseus with some countermagick to protect him from Circe's power before he pays her a visit. Odysseus is bathed by her handmaidens in a giant cauldron and attends a feast with her, but does not eat. It is clear that he is impervious to her potions and charms, and he draws his sword as if to attack. Upon realizing she has no magical power over him, Circe manages to convince him that she means him no further harm and will instead help him. She returns his men back to their natural state, and they all spend a year on the island. During much of that time, Odysseus shares Circe's bed. When it is time to set off, Circe suggests alternative routes for them that will be safer and also gives Odysseus crucial advice he will need to navigate the Underworld.

Symbolism: The Odyssey mentions a beautiful cauldron in the framework of the bathing of the hero before he is presented to Circe, but it is generally accepted/assumed that perhaps Circe also brews her potions in this cauldron, which is perhaps why the bath is mentioned and presented as part of the evidence that the countermagick was effective. But it's specifically *not* the cauldron that is the root of her power, but rather her knowledge of herbs, potions, and poisons.

Cauldron Consideration: Our tools are not the source of our power; they simply aid us. True power comes from the knowledge we acquire as we determine to be forever learning. Also, trying to constantly exert your will over others can only work for so long and will eventually wear you down. Focus on change within yourself, and magick will happen faster.

Medea and Her Cauldron of Rejuvenation

Medea is a complicated figure in Greek myth, a femme fatale and the source of much controversy and strife. She is connected to magick as the niece of Circe, being the daughter of Circe's brother Aeetes. Medea is best known from Euripides's play named after her, where she supposedly takes revenge on her husband Jason's betrayal by killing their children. Our cauldron story predates all of that.

The Story: We first encounter Medea aiding Jason in getting the Golden Fleece from her father, Aeetes. After securing the treasure, Jason took Medea with him and fell in love with her. Knowing of her potion skills, cunning, and powers of rejuvenation, Jason asked her to help his aged father, Aeson. According to legend, she drew out all of the old man's blood and replaced it with herbal juices, returning his health and vigor and spreading her fame far and wide. The daughters of Pelias petitioned Medea to reveal her secret so they could invigorate their father too—not knowing that Medea had a bone to pick with him. She agreed to demonstrate. Warming up her cauldron, she created quite a spectacle, tossing in herbs and muttering incantations, the room filling with smoke. She cut the throat of an old ram and put it in the cauldron. Suddenly a young lamb emerged out of the cauldron! The daughters, falling prey to Medea's deception and believing they now understood how to give new life to their father, tried to recreate the ritual on their own, with disastrous results: they ended up unwittingly murdering their own father.

Medea's cauldron

Symbolism: Evident throughout the many variations of stories about Medea is that she clearly did know her herbs, potions, and power. The cauldron in this particular myth is the site of trickery, illusion, and sleight of hand, but that doesn't mean everything she did was fake. The spells brewed in the cauldron could definitely bring the power of rejuvenation—if Medea was on your side.

Cauldron Consideration: Practitioners of magick are capable of both cunning and conning—some of it is real and some of it is show. Be careful whom you place your trust in, as they may not always have your best intentions in mind. Nor do you need to reveal all of your secrets simply because someone asks it of you.

The Cailleach's Cauldron

Our last myth centers on the Gaelic goddess Cailleach—an ancestral deity of nature and weather, having dominion over the land, sea, plants, and animals. Interestingly enough, a specific landmark is explained by her myth.

The Story: The Cailleach, whose name translates to "old woman" or "hag," has been revered throughout the United Kingdom for as long as anyone can remember. Because she is associated with nature and weather, there are many geographical locations tied to the numerous variations of her. For this myth, we're focusing on the particular one concerning the whirlpool of Corryvreckan (*Coire Bhreacain:* "cauldron of the plaid"). The Scots say that the Cailleach brings in winter by washing her big plaid in the whirlpool. Before the washing takes place, a loud windy storm is heard from miles around for up to three days solid before the "cauldron boils." After the washing is done, the plaid is pure white. The Corryvreckan is one of only seven major whirlpools in the world.

Symbolism: In this myth, the actions of a goddess are used to explain the workings of a real-world geographic oddity and the changing of the seasons. The suggestion that the plaid turns pure white after its three days of washing as winter advances could represent both physically and spiritually cleaning out the old year and beginning anew.

Cauldron Consideration: Sometimes the transformation of the physical actually reflects a transformation of the mind or spirit. Inversely, cleansing the mind and spirit can also lead to purification of the body. What baggage are you holding on to that's holding you back?

Not Just for the Ladies

For as many times as I've seen the cauldron claimed as an object of the Goddess, there sure are quite a few cauldron myths that focus on men and gods. Why is that? Could it be that the cauldron does indeed symbolically represent the nether regions of a woman, therefore explaining why men chase after them? More likely, the cauldron was seen as an object of power and mystery for both men and women. There is indeed evidence throughout the world that cooking wasn't (and isn't) always deemed "women's work." The ability of a leader to feed their people as well as guests on a grand scale was cause for celebration and honor, as suggested by the Celtic feasting cauldrons discussed earlier in this chapter. Maybe the heroes and gods of old also enjoyed cooking up a good barbeque themselves? Or perhaps our ancestors recognized the role that alcohol often plays in freeing up "inspiration"?

The Dagda's Cauldron

The Dagda is the Celtic god of the earth and "All-Father" and the leader of the Tuatha de Danann ("people of the goddess Danu"), a supernatural race of people. He is said to be the son of Danu and the father of Brigid and Aengus, and is married to the Morrigan. His name means "the good god" or "the good one," and he presides over many things, including life, death, war, banquets, artistry, and music.

The Story: The *Undry*, the Cauldron of Plenty, is one of the four treasures of the Tuatha de Danann. (The other three treasures are the Spear of Lugh, the Stone of Fal, and the Sword of Light.) As you might expect from the god of banquets, no one ever went away hungry from his feasts, and this cauldron was a veritable cornucopia, producing a never-ending supply of food. As if that weren't enough in the food department, the Dagda was also in possession of two magical pigs—one that's constantly roasting and one that never stops growing—and a fruit tree that is always producing. The Dagda also had a magical harp that could summon the seasons, and a huge club that could kill nine men in one swipe from one end, but could bring them back from death from the other end.

Symbolism: The possessions of the Dagda all represent what it means to be a good father/leader: having the tools to feed your people and protect them, as well as having the mystical territories of the gods—to be able to take or give life, to control the weather and the seasons. As evidenced by our historical cauldrons, feasting was a huge deal. It not only was a show of power and brought the community together, but it also meant that in an uncertain world the people would be provided for.

Cauldron Consideration: See your cauldron as an opportunity to bring together the community and provide for everyone's well-being. Whether it's part of a magical group working or a meal that you will make to share with friends or family, your cauldron not only provides for the body physically but is also beneficial for the mind and soul.

Odin and the Well of Urd

Following along with the theme of father gods, we come to Odin, a major player in Germanic and Norse mythology. In contrast to the Dagda, Odin is far more interested in searching for wisdom than setting up feasts.

The Story: Behold Yggdrasil, an enormous tree that is at the center of the cosmos, holding in its branches and roots the Nine Worlds—where the gods, humans, and all other beings live. Yggdrasil grows out of the Well of Urd (*Urd* means "fate" or "destiny"). Within the Well of Urd reside the Norns, a trio of wise women who carve into the tree the destinies of all beings and draw water from the Well to care for Yggdrasil. The carved destinies are not set in stone, but rather—indicative of them being marked into a living tree—every being has power to influence their own destiny.

Odin is said to have consulted the Norns and visited the Well of Urd on numerous occasions. I have chosen two specific stories that I feel best correlate with the cauldron myths while also giving us insight into Odin's personality. The first involves Odin wanting to know the wisdom of the runes, which also reside with the Norns in the Well. The runes reveal themselves only to those who prove themselves worthy of such knowledge. To accomplish this, Odin began by hanging himself by his feet from a branch of Yggdrasil, so that he was positioned to stare down into the waters of the Well. He pierced himself with a spear and hung from the great tree for nine days and nine nights, hovering between life and death, until the runes finally deemed him worthy.

The other story involves a journey to Mimir's Well, which is speculated to also be the Well of Urd. Mimir, whose name means "the rememberer," is a mysterious guardian of the Well. (Mimir's gender tends to change depending on the account, possibly referring to one or more of the Norns who occupy the same space or another person altogether at different times, so I have chosen to refer to them in third gender.) Their knowledge of all things was said to be unparalleled, primarily since they drank from the Well they guarded—the waters of which were said to be imbued with knowledge. Upon his arrival, Odin asked Mimir for a drink, but was told that he must offer up an eye in order to do so. Odin obliged, gouging out one of his own eyes and sacrificing it to the Well, and then was able to partake of the waters.

Odin hanging from Yggdrasil,
staring down into the Well of Urd

53

Symbolism: The Well of Urd, while not usually described as a cauldron, satisfies many of its aspects: containing, transforming, divining, nourishing. In order to partake of the Well's gifts and gain its knowledge, sacrifices must be made. It's also interesting to note that Odin gave up his physical eye for another form of being able to see and perceive the world.

Cauldron Consideration: In order to gain great knowledge, we must be willing to make sacrifices, for wisdom is never gained easily. While that typically does not involve sacrificing body parts, it does mean investing time and effort, as well as exercising patience. We must remember that the universe owes us nothing and demands our respect.

Thor and the Cauldron of Hymir

We're going to travel down the family tree for our next myth featuring Odin's son Thor. While his father is thirsty for knowledge and cosmic insight, Thor is more of an athletic and sporting kind of guy, focused on competition, battles of strength, and getting his way.

The Story: Our cauldron story starts off with Thor and other godly friends who have been out hunting and now would like to imbibe. Through divination, they decide the best place to feast and slake their thirst is at the home of Aegir (whose name means "ocean"). Aegir is annoyed when Thor's party shows up at his door. He tells Thor that in order for him to help them, the gods must bring him a cauldron large enough to brew ale in. They search without luck, until Týr (god of war) conveniently remembers that his father, Hymir (a giant), owns a cauldron that measures a mile wide. So Thor and Týr head off to visit his family, which is complicated because the gods and the giants are at odds with each other. But Týr's mother is sympathetic and helps them secure the cauldron.

At Hymir's home, a feast is held in which Thor eats two oxen by himself (all the rest gathered eat one among them). In the morning, Hymir and Thor go fishing to replenish the household—after Thor rips the head off of Hymir's best ox to use for bait. Far out at sea, Hymir catches two whales, while Thor manages to hook with his ox-head bait Jörmungandr, the Midgard serpent that circles the world. He reels it in, and with the serpent thrashing about, Thor tries to smash it with his hammer, Mjöllnir. Frightened by this display, Hymir cuts the line, allowing the serpent to escape. Thor is suitably angered and Hymir embarrassed. They row back to shore in silence. Upon arriving, Hymir suggests that Thor help him carry the whales or drag the boat up the shore. Thor picks up the boat, the whales, *and* Hymir and carries them back to the farm.

Now thoroughly humiliated, Hymir challenges Thor to a test of strength that involves trying to smash a crystal goblet. First Thor throws it against a stone pillar, but it is the pillar that is destroyed, not the goblet. Týr's mother suggests throwing it at Hymir's head, which is even more solid than rock, and the goblet is smashed. Hymir concedes and gives the cauldron to Thor and Týr. Týr is unable to even lift the cauldron, but Thor easily picks it up and hoists it onto his shoulder, and they start back on their way to Aegir's. The loss of Hymir's cauldron does not sit well with the rest of the giants, who try to attack them, but Thor kills them all with his hammer. They arrive back at Aegir's, who brews the ale, and since then, every winter the gods go to drink at his hall.

Symbolism: In this myth, the cauldron appears to be mainly a questing vehicle, designed to move the story along. What is special about it is its unusually large size, but the cauldron otherwise doesn't seem to have any unique magical properties. However, when we consider the anger of the other giants over the loss of Hymir's cauldron, we are reminded of the pride and importance of the cauldron within a community. To take away that cauldron is to steal that powerful communal symbol.

Cauldron Consideration: In reading the tales of Thor, I can't help but be aghast at his constant bumbling and breaches of hospitality. It's important to be respectful not only of ourselves but also of other people's bodies, beliefs, and belongings.

Stirring the Cauldron:
A Heathen's Cauldron

THE CAULDRON, OR kettle, played a very important part in Norse religion. It is the vessel in which the meat of the holy feast (in the old days, the beast slain as a gift to the gods and goddesses) is seethed. The word *ketill* ("kettle") and the name *Katla* (which derives from *ketill*) were very common in the Viking Age and almost certainly first had a ritual meaning. Compounds such as *Þórkell* ("Þórr's kettle"—a man's name) were also common. In *Grímnismál*, Óðinn mentions that the ways between the worlds are opened "when kettles are heaved off the fire." Grønbech argues strongly for the cauldrons seething the sacrificial feast as embodiments of the might of the three great Wells of Wyrd, Mímir, and Hvergelmir (II, 290–97). In Snorri's description of the brewing of the mead, *Óðroerir* ("Wod-Stirrer" or "Inspiration-Stirrer"), he says that Kvasir's blood was put in two tubs and one kettle, and it was the kettle itself that bore the name Óðroerir (while the tubs were called Són and Boðn); it was clearly the chief magical vessel.

Cauldrons are mentioned a few times in the lore (the collection of myths, poems, stories, and histories that remain from pre-Christian Scandinavia) that we base our religious practices on. When cauldrons are discussed, they are associated with the brewing of alcoholic beverages, either the mead of inspiration or beer. The sea god Aegir is said to have a cauldron a mile wide in his hall under the ocean that he uses to brew enormous quantities of beer so that all of the gods will come and feast with him. These beverages are central to the main rituals we modern-day Asatruar participate in: Blot and Sumbel. These rituals are sacred drinking rituals in which a beverage, usually mead but sometimes beer or another beverage, depending on which god is being honored, are poured into a drinking horn.

For Blot, the horn is passed around the group and toasts to the god being honored are spoken over it, and thus the words enter the Well of Wyrd. Once the toasts are complete, the then-sacred mead is offered to the god as a libation: "From the gods, to the earth, to us. From us, to the earth, to the gods. A gift for a Gift." In Sumbel, the horn is passed around the group for toasts to a god, hero, or ancestor; boasts and oaths can also be shared among the folk at this time.

In my local Heathen community, we are lucky enough to include in our kin and close friends several excellent brewers of beer and mead. Hospitality is a very important concept in Asatru. To provide good hospitality means offering your guests the best you have available. Having brewers in our midst allows us to offer our friends, and our gods, an array of amazing beer and mead, much better than anything that could be bought, brewed with the finest ingredients, and, most importantly, brewed with the intention that it be a proper offering to the gods and an accompaniment to sacred feasting that takes place after Blot. Our appreciation for the talent of these good folks, as well as our familiarity with the labor-intensive work they do, has led us to honor Aegir as a god of brewers. We hold an annual Blot to honor Aegir. Brewing is incorporated as part of the Blot preparation. Kindred members and friends will brew together during the day, gathering around large steaming brew kettles and sampling previous batches.

As the brewing winds down, we'll gather by the fire pit to offer blot (literally meaning "sacrifice") to Aegir. The offerings take many forms—I once saw an entire batch of wort (unfermented beer) sacrificed by breaking the glass carboy with a hammer. Other times brewing ingredients, like freshly harvested hops or a full recipe's worth of malted grain, are sacrificed to the fire for Aegir. Through honoring the brewers' god, we also honor their work, and the ways in which the fruits of

Gather Round—
The Cauldron in History & Myth

their labor serve to bind the community together. We have a saying that is often said in jest, though it does contain some truth: "The Frith is in the froth!," meaning the good feelings of peace and connectedness we share as a community spring, at least in part, from the good beer and mead we share. Lest we get carried away, the Havamal contains several passages that warn of the dangers found in over-indulgence, reminding us that a wise person possesses self-control!

Sarah Bennett
A Northeast Heathen
and member of Raven
Kindred North •
RavenNorth.org

The Questing Cauldrons

There is so much convoluted overlap among our next group of cauldron stories that I like to describe them collectively as "these guys who keep stealing the same darn cauldron." As with any myth, they all start in one place, and as they are told and retold, the details shift and change to reflect the region and society in which they are told. Other people like certain parts of a myth and then add those bits to their own mythology. With the United Kingdom and surrounding areas being a fairly small region with a long history of exchange and warfare, it's easy to see why so many of these stories have multiple variations. Countless volumes have been written trying to explain and explore these myths over the last several hundred years, so I'm going to focus more on identifying the powers, meaning, and symbolism behind these cauldrons.

The Cauldron of Dyrnwch the Giant

One of the Thirteen Treasures of the Island of Britain is the Cauldron of Dyrnwch the Giant (Pair Dyrnwch Gawr). This cauldron is said to be able to discriminate between brave men and cowards by way of an unusual cooking test. If a coward were to try and cook his meal in it, it would not boil. Inversely, the meal of a brave man would certainly boil quickly.

The Cauldron Born Soldiers

The Story: King Arthur requests the cauldron from the giant Dyrnwch, who refuses to give it up. Arthur travels to Ireland to visit him, and Dyrnwch refuses again. One of Arthur's men seizes the cauldron, kills the giant, and starts an epic battle. They manage to escape back to Britain with the cauldron and other spoils.

The Symbolism: Here we have a unique power for a cauldron: it tests the bravery of men, deeming who is to be worthy of the feast. This adds another interesting layer to the symbolism of the feasting cauldrons, which were a show of feeding everyone. In this particular tale, those who are not brave do not deserve food, nor honor and respect. We see a distinct shift from the idea of winning or earning a cauldron to instead taking it brutally by force—creating a new kind of "bravery."

Cauldron Consideration: Much of the Arthurian romances are tied up with the integration of Christianity in the region, but the resulting stories don't seem to say much for the older religions nor the new. So in considering this myth, I believe it's best to harness the power of actually working to do good versus claiming it by name only.

Bran and the Pair Dadeni (The Cauldron of Rebirth)

The cauldron in this story (and its many variations) is able to bring people back to life, particularly warriors, which reminds us of the decorated panel on the Gundestrup Cauldron illustrating this same scene. With so much warring going on, this cauldron's ability to provide a deathless army makes it an object of much desire. It also reminds us of the myth of the Holy Grail—the cup that caught the blood of Jesus Christ and supposedly grants anyone who drinks from it everlasting life. However, while it may seem similar to the Holy Grail, there is a significant catch regarding its life-giving properties. Anyone reborn from this cauldron cannot speak: "I will give unto thee a cauldron the property of which is, that if one of the men be slain today, and be cast therein, tomorrow he will be as well as ever he was at his best, except that he will not regain his speech." (This is from "Branwen the Daughter of Llyr," *The Mabinogion*, translated by Lady Charlotte Guest.)

The Story: Bran is a Welsh king who provides hospitality to a giant and giantess who are fleeing death and destruction in Ireland. Out of gratitude, they bestow upon him the gift of a magic cauldron that can resurrect dead warriors. Bran in turn gives it to his sister Branwen on the occasion of her marriage to the King of Ireland and to smooth over some tension. This union is a problematic match in many ways, and Bran and his army set out to get the cauldron (and his sister) back.

During the ensuing battle, the Irish use the cauldron to keep reanimating their soldiers until one of the Welsh knights hides among the dead. He is tossed into the cauldron, where he bursts it from the inside, both destroying it and killing himself in the process. Only seven knights return home, and Bran himself is mortally wounded by a poisoned spear (à la the Fisher

King in Arthurian legend). In some versions of the story, Bran asks that his head be cut off and it becomes an oracle, having the ability to speak and prophesy on its own.

Symbolism: In this story, Bran is given a great gift in exchange for his hospitality. He unfortunately gives it (and his sister) away, putting it in the hands of the people from whom its original owners were fleeing. Not only does this lead to his undoing and his sister's deep unhappiness, but the cauldron is also destroyed in the process. Also, what does it mean for the soldiers to be reborn without being able to talk? Does that make them simply reanimated corpses, or are they just unable to tell of their journey past the doors of death? It's hard to say whether this cauldron truly gives the gift of life again or simply makes for endless battle fodder. It's the kind of rejuvenation a king would want for his army but not for himself.

Cauldron Consideration: Sometimes we have a hard time truly valuing the gifts we are given, and we accidentally squander them to appease others. Also, we may think the grass is greener on the other side and fail to enjoy what we have before us. Take time to savor your own gifts and find the beauty in them, like a delicious hot cup of tea.

The Cauldron of Annwn

The last of the questing cauldrons is the Cauldron of Annwn, which is known as a cauldron of both rebirth and inspiration. Annwn is the Otherworld or Underworld (Annwn translates to "very deep" in Welsh), ruled by Arawn, who has many similar qualities to the Lord of the Wild Hunt, emphasizing the death/Underworld aspect. Annwn is said to be a paradise, full of beauty and eternal youth and free from disease and hunger. It's also been equated with Avalon in later Arthurian tales.

I suspect that the Cauldron of Annwn is possibly the all-myth cauldron that pulls them all together. As a cauldron of inspiration (its name is quite similar to Awen), it seems to be connected to Ceridwen's cauldron. It's said to be located in the Underworld within the waters, so it not only harkens to the Well of Urd and divination but also connects to rejuvenation and rebirth, like Bran's cauldron. In lines 13–17 of the poem "Preiddeu Annwn," or "The Spoils of Annwfyn," as translated by Sarah Higley, we're told of King Arthur and his knights raiding the Underworld, in search of a magical cauldron attended by nine maidens:

> *My poetry, from the cauldron it was uttered.*
> *From the breath of nine maidens it was kindled.*
> *The cauldron of the chief of Annwfyn:*
> *what is its fashion?*
> *A dark ridge around its border and pearls.*
> *It does not boil the food of a coward;*
> *it has not been destined.*

Here we can also see a connection to the unique cooking quirk of Dyrnwch the Giant's cauldron. Interestingly, some translations of the poem have replaced *chief* with *head*, which has led some people to believe that this refers to the head of Bran. But if we think back to those historical feasting cauldrons, connected to their chieftains, that very literal connection seems rather out of place, not to mention that Bran's cauldron was destroyed. *Chief* means the leader of the Annwn, not his head. Of the pearls described around the cauldron's rim, we could see them as the proverbial pearls of wisdom or the embodied essence of dream and memory. Last but not least, we have those nine maidens and their breath that kindles the cauldron, which could refer to both poetry and magick. Nine, as the root of 3 x 3, is certainly a magical number that surfaces again and again throughout Celtic lore.

Symbolism and Cauldron Consideration: The Cauldron of Annwn really is the all-cauldron and holder of mysteries. It clearly is not of this world, but still manages to inspire us. Its potential to give new life can send us on new journeys and quests, but it's not simply a trophy to be won. If we step away from the pursuits of strife and conquest, there lies an opportunity to rest, rejuvenate, and be reborn.

A Last Look at the Questing Cauldrons

As I've already established, I'm not entirely convinced that the cauldron automatically and symbolically has something to do with women or goddesses. In most of the questing tales, many of the cauldrons aren't owned by women, nor are women directly linked with that part of the story. But I also cannot deny that there's definitely an undercurrent of "we're men on a sacred duty, we'll take what we want" in many of the stories, and there are plenty of myths where that entitlement naturally includes women's bodies and their mysteries. Was that attitude original to those myths, or were they themes that were added in later centuries by those of a different social mind?

There's also certainly a joke in here somewhere about how men chasing cauldrons is really about men chasing after women. Humanity definitely has had a long fascination with sex and procreation—does eternal life perhaps refer to ensuring your lineage through offspring rather than living forever? There are modern scholars who theorize that the Holy Grail was not a cup or chalice but was actually a symbol for Mary Magdelene, who according to some accounts was the wife of Jesus and the mother of his children. Whatever gifts the cauldron may bring, it is definitely a symbol that inspires the human spirit.

Trial by Fire: The Boiling Cauldrons

The last of our cauldron myths feature boiling cauldrons. There are many references in dozens of myths from around the world where there is a trial or miracle involving a bubbling cauldron. Sometimes there's an unfortunate and untimely death, and either part or all of the subject is immersed in a special cauldron and is either reformed as an infant or restored to their original state. There are a few examples of this happening in Greek myth, such as Dionysus, who was attacked, killed, and boiled in a cauldron by two Titans. His heart was salvaged in time by Zeus, who was able to recreate Dionysus. There's also the "trial by cauldron," which shows up often in Russian and Slavic folklore, such as in the stories of the Firebird, where the hero is given a magical potion to withstand being boiled alive, while his enemy attempting to do the same meets an unfortunate end.

The Symbolism: Since the cauldron has been an integral part of civilization for many hundreds of years, people were familiar with both its benefits and hazards. There's also the undertone of the horrors of cannibalism, again easily pictured by people who would cook meat in their pots. Being able to survive such an ordeal showed amazing strength and possession of great power or magick. These cauldrons are not special because they enabled rebirth, but by the fact that the subjects survived them at all.

Cauldron Consideration: What can help can also harm, if you're not careful. Take care to prepare properly when working with your cauldron so you don't get burned—either physically or by a poor choice of magical working.

Pop-Culture Cauldrons and Mythology

We can see that the cauldron has been a part of our mythology for thousands of years, but that doesn't make it all ancient history. I think it's important to give a nod to the presence of the cauldron in our modern-day mythology too. From the infamous trio of witches brewing away in Shakespeare's *Macbeth*, to Disney's Mickey Mouse as *The Sorcerer's Apprentice*, to Merlin and Madam Mim in *The Sword in the Stone*—and, of course, the standard size 2 cauldron of Harry Potter's world—the cauldron still fires our imagination and helps to create a whole new age of mythology.

In a book this size, I couldn't even begin to start listing all of the cauldrons in mythology without needing to write a whole new book! So when you see a cauldron on TV or in a movie, or when you read about a cauldron or listen to a podcast about one, I encourage you take a moment to think about how it's being used and what possible symbolism is there. Considering modern society's deep fascination with Witches, it looks like the myth of the cauldron will continue to live on and inspire us for generations to come.

chapter
3

The Practical Cauldron

Now that we've explored the historical uses and mythic roots of the cauldron, let's consider the modern-day Witch. Over the course of history, Witches have had to walk the line between having special, ritual-specific tools and having tools that can easily double for both daily use and ritual needs. For the most part, owning special items for just magick is not that big a deal (unless you have to be in the proverbial broom closet), though nowadays the cauldron does tend to look out of place in most homes! To get a good idea of the options that are available to you, we'll consider the differences between shapes and makes of cauldrons, as well as buying one versus making your own.

The Shapely Cauldron

Cauldrons have a fairly standard shape, but can vary in their design. When handling hot items, I feel it's important to make sure your vessel is designed to do the kind of job you need it for, is stable and won't tip over, and is easy for you to handle and maneuver.

Body—Curved vs. Straight Sides: The rounded horizontal design makes for easier stirring and quicker evaporation. A more vertically oriented design, with straight sides, can make stirring more difficult and cuts back on evaporation.

Feet vs. No Feet: Some cauldrons have a standard tripod of feet, which is superior for stability and air flow—versus a cauldron that has none. The latter is designed more to be hung and/or placed on a separate specialized tripod.

Handles: Lastly, note what sort of handles the cauldron has. Are they easy for you to grasp, or are they just holes for a separate, single large handle? Are they molded on as part of the cauldron or are they separate? Molded-on handles tend to heat up more quickly, but separate ones aren't always attached as firmly and may give when you lift it if there's a lot of weight inside of the cauldron.

Makes and Metals

Cauldrons can be made from a vast array of materials. The most common kind is metal, but even within that category you have quite a number of options to consider. Let's take a look at the strengths and weaknesses of some of the most popular metals, as well as their attributed magical properties.

Iron

The most popular kind of cauldrons are cast-iron ones, which are made of an alloy of iron and carbon that can be readily cast in a mold. They're hard, durable, and slow to heat, but when the cauldron finally gets hot, it stays hot for quite some time.

Magical Properties

One of the most abundant elements in the universe, iron is ruled by the planet Mars and is considered to be masculine in nature. There's a fair bit of folklore from multiple regions (especially the UK) that speaks of iron repelling the Fey, spirits, and some forms of magick. Since iron is in nearly everything (including blood), anti-Fey and anti-magick mentalities about it are probably rooted in human use of iron for weapons—which would logically be cause for much distaste. I wouldn't overthink it, but if you're looking to work with certain energies known to be driven away by iron, then perhaps consider another metal option for your cauldron.

Tip for Cast-Iron Cauldrons

If you'd like to speed up the heating process of your cast-iron cauldron, place it in the oven for 15–20 minutes at 200–300°F, then remove it with a potholder and get started!

Copper

Copper has been utilized for cauldron making for quite a long time. It has excellent thermal and electrical conductivity, good strength, and good workability and is resistant to corrosion. One of the most important properties of copper (as well as its resulting alloys, such as brass and bronze) is its ability to fight bacteria. Considering how recently we've come to understand bacteria, it's remarkable to note that copper has been involved in many kinds of water-purification processes for thousands of years.

Magical Properties

Copper is ruled by the planet Venus, so it is considered to be feminine in energy and connected to healing processes. If you have a particular talent for or interest in healing work, a copper cauldron may be the one for you.

Bronze

Bronze is an alloy that consists primarily of copper, with the addition of other ingredients (typically tin), making an alloy that is much harder than copper alone. Bronze is often used in the construction of sculptures for its strength and beauty, and in musical instruments for its sound. It's also utilized for nautical applications because it's resistant to corrosion.

Magical Properties

Being an alloy of copper and tin, bronze possesses characteristics of both. Tin is ruled by Jupiter, is considered masculine in nature, and is associated with divination. So if copper is feminine and tin is masculine, that makes bronze gender-neutral!

Brass

Brass is an alloy that consists of copper with zinc added, which improves its strength. Brass has an additional appeal, because with its deep yellow color it resembles gold. It also is used to manufacture musical instruments.

Magical Properties

Brass is ruled by the Sun and has long been associated with money spells since it resembles gold. It is also considered to be good for protection work and healing.

Silver

When you see a silver cauldron, it's probably silver-plated instead of being pure silver, which would be very costly! If it's plated, then the underneath is probably polished steel (making it an iron alloy). If it looks like silver but isn't marked, it's probably a variation of pewter, which has a low melting point, and if it contains lead, it is especially *not* safe to use for a lot of things! Silver is definitely a thing of beauty, and the phrase "silver cauldron" does make a great book title—but it's not a good working metal for daily use, though it is fine for decorative, special, and other non-active purposes.

Magical Properties
Silver is ruled by the Moon and is associated with love, dreams, peace, protection, wealth, and psychic powers.

The Non-Metals

Occasionally you will find cauldrons made of ceramic, glass, crystal, stone, wood, resin, and other kinds of plastics. These typically are ornamental in nature, so their use is limited. Ceramic cauldrons can be heated and used for many cooking applications (though notably for oven use versus stove use), but they aren't effective at conducting heat or as durable as metal cauldrons. Leaded glass, crystal, and ornamental glasses can be very beautiful and definitely add flash and beauty, but unless they're specifically marked for heating (like Pyrex glass), avoid directly heating them (as cookware) or using them for charcoal disks.

Stone cauldrons can be used for mixing, containing, and other non-heat activities, but I would exercise caution in using them for heated applications, even if you're only using a candle to generate the heat. Using the vessel for cooking or charcoal may cause it to crack and break if there are any impurities in the rock. One advantage of using a stone cauldron would be if the magical properties of the stone align with your practice/devotion. Wooden bowls are beautiful and can make great serving dishes, but for obvious reasons you don't want to cook with them or use heat with them in any way. In the "Making Your Own Cauldron" section later in this chapter, I've included some ideas for paper cauldrons, though these are meant to be a one-use composting option—and obviously are not meant to hold much or withstand the heat of a flame! Lastly, especially near Halloween, you'll see many a plastic and resin cauldron adorning store shelves. They're wonderful for decoration and kitsch, but that's about it. Say *nope* to plastic for practical use.

Choosing the Right Cauldron for You

With so many options, how do you pick the right cauldron for you? There are some important things to consider before making your selection.

First, Do You Even Need a Cauldron?

There is often a strong pull to get "all the stuff" right away when you start along a path, and there are plenty of folks happy to sell you those things. But as you'll read in chapter 8, you may already have items in your household that suit your needs just fine. I'm a big fan of "use what you have," but I also can't deny the allure of magical tools. I have multiple wands, chalices, Tarot decks, blades, and, of course, cauldrons—but not because I use all of them. Rather, I collect them for their artistry, meaning, and beauty. I also have plenty of mundane items that I can repurpose for magical use at any time.

Some paths also teach that you should keep mundane and magical items separate to retain the purity of the spiritual energy. From a commonsense perspective, when it comes to mixing potions and burning items, you're probably not going to want to use the same vessel in which you burn incense for boiling pasta. To reference the kosher guidelines of Judaism as an example, those rules were put in place to keep people healthy and alive, not strictly because it was a commandment from a deity. So it is quite nice to have certain items that you designate for very specific and special uses.

Lastly, I think you'd be hard-pressed to find a Witch who doesn't have even a tiny bit of romance for the idea of the cauldron. Even if we don't have a lot of space or much in the way of practical applications for a cauldron, their mythology and symbolism call to us. So if it makes you happy (and probably a bit gleeful), why not?

What Kind Should You Get?

In order to determine what kind and size of cauldron you need, consider what you plan to use it for. Will you be cooking in it? Scrying? Burning? Cleansing?

If you're going to be preparing or storing food and/or drink in your cauldron, then you'll want to get one that is food-safe and can withstand heat and cold. Your best option is going to be a true cast-iron cauldron that is seasoned (or can be), with proper handles, base, and lid.

Likewise, if you're planning to use your cauldron to burn candles or incense or start any sort of fire, you'll want to make sure it's fireproof and easy to handle and has a well-fitting lid.

If you want to use your cauldron for divination, then you will want to look for a finish that inspires you. Some people prefer a nice black cauldron, while others like the designs a glaze makes inside of a bowl or the way light refracts in a crystal or glass bowl.

If you have a specific ritual use in mind, then you'll want to see if any particular metal works best (such as a copper cauldron versus an iron one for working with the Fey). If you're going mainly for decoration, then the world is your oyster.

What Size Do You Need?

Tiny cauldrons are adorable and giant cauldrons are the envy of many a Witch, but how useful are they? If the tiny cauldron can't even hold a tealight candle or charcoal disk, and you wish to do candle or smoke magick, then it's not going to be very functional or safe. But if that tiny cauldron is for storing a special momento, crystal, or pendant, then it will be perfect. If you live in a small apartment with no access to a yard, then a giant cauldron won't be much more than a decoration taking up a lot of space. But if you live in a good-size house and have a large family (or coven), are into cooking big meals and/or brewing, and have a secure outdoor location or large indoor hearth for the giant cauldron, then it will be perfect for you. Be realistic about your needs, uses, and space, and you'll find a cauldron that's just right for you.

How Much Should You Pay for It?

How much should a cauldron cost? It really varies depending on what kind and size you want to get. If it's something that's handmade by an artisan, then you're looking at making an investment for a unique piece. If it's mass-manufactured, then you've got the advantage of checking online to compare sizes, makes, models, and pricing, and they can vary from a few dollars to thousands. Just be sure to read the information carefully to make sure you're getting the right cauldron for your needs.

If there's an occult or metaphysical shop near you, I would recommend checking out what they have. It may cost a few more dollars there than purchasing it online (since they also need to cover their overhead costs that many online businesses don't have to worry about), but you'll save on shipping and you can handle the cauldron in person and see if you like it. Oftentimes, if there's something specific you're looking for, they can special order it for you. Plus you're supporting a local small business, which is always awesome!

> *Cauldron Cents:* Don't settle for the first cauldron you find if it's not a good fit for your needs or your budget.

Making Your Own Cauldron

There are several ways you can go about making your own cauldron, from crafting it from scratch to personalizing it.

Iron and Metal

Forge your own cauldron! I really wish I could include a how-to section on blacksmithing and metalwork, but unless you're already familiar with those techniques, you're going to need a lot more than this book to get started. However, wanting to make your own metal cauldron from scratch is a great reason to sign up for a blacksmithing or metalworking class. Check out your local community college, art center, or makerspace for classes where you can begin to learn these techniques. I know metalsmiths who have booths at Renaissance faires and regularly offer workshops, so maybe you already know an artisan you could learn from. You could also learn to make vessels out of copper, silver, and other malleable metals in a basic jewelry/light metals class.

It's *very* important to understand that you will be investing a large amount of time (and most likely money) in pursuit of learning how to make your own metal cauldron from scratch. It takes practice to create a vessel that will suit your needs, so don't expect to make a great cauldron in a single day. But if this is something that inspires you, then perhaps you'll be on your way to learning a new art or trade.

Now, let's say you are indeed already an accomplished blacksmith or metalworker—then this is right up your alley! With technique and experience under your belt, the next consideration is what process (casting, forging, or dapping) and what metal you would like to use to construct your cauldron. Check out the kinds of cauldrons section to consider the magical properties and pros and cons of each kind of material—but if you work with a specific kind of metal, that will most likely be your best option for starters.

Ceramic

Another option for making your own cauldron is to make it out of clay, which you may find more accessible than metalworking. It's typically easier to find a ceramics studio at an art center, college, or shop. As with metalworking, though, it does take time to develop skill working the clay to get a result you'll be happy with, though cost-wise it tends to be less expensive. A bag of clay is pretty affordable, and you can rent kiln space pretty cheap (or even build a backyard kiln). There are many varieties of clays out there—white, red, low-fire, high-fire, porcelain, stoneware, etc.—so if you're new to ceramics, I recommend signing up for classes and finding out what kind of clay you like to work with first, as well as what kinds of kilns are accessible to you through the studio. I suggest starting with a hand-building class versus throwing on the wheel right away. You can learn a multitude of techniques to create a decent cauldron-shaped vessel, along with handles, lid, and more, without ever having to learn how to use a potter's wheel. In a class, you'll learn what mistakes to avoid, how to make sure your lid will fit your piece, and how to properly glaze your piece. Soon you'll be making a variety of dishes, bowls, and holders to match as well! Just be sure to avoid using glazes with lead in them if you plan to eat or drink out of your creations.

If you're uneasy about telling the instructor that you want to make a cauldron, focus on what you want to do with your vessel. Is it for holding liquid? Burning incense? Making a fire pot? Do you want to be able to microwave it or use it in a dishwasher? A knowledgeable instructor will be able to help you make good choices in structure, medium, and glazing to meet all of these needs without you needing to divulge any spiritual or magical details.

Note: Polymer clays and similar kinds of humanmade clay that you can bake in your home oven are best avoided for use as a functioning cauldron. They're not made to withstand high heat, can release dangerous fumes and chemicals, and rarely are safe for using with food and drink. They truly are for decorative use only!

Paper and Paper Mache

Maybe you're looking for a strictly decorative cauldron for a ritual play, or something that could be buried or burned all together? Then you might want to consider paper-molding or paper mache for your cauldron. With paper mache, all you need is water and flour (some recipes recommend water and white glue), paper (newspapers, paper towels, etc.), and a shape to use to get started on. A balloon, bowl, or two-liter bottle of soda can make a great base. If you wish to get more elaborate, check out papermaking, which is a wonderful process for crafty folk. You can include strips of fabric and fiber, add herb parts (petals, leaves, etc.) to your pulp that correlate with your spellcraft, or include seeds that will later sprout when planted. Check out www.ultimatepapermache.com for a wealth of recipes and ideas.

3-D Printing

If you're a tech wizard and into 3-D printing (or live near a makerspace that offers classes in 3-D printing), then you could conceivably design and print your own cauldron! At this time, though, most consumer-level printers use plastic and resin—not ideal for anything involving fire. You could send your design to a company that specializes in 3-D printing in metal or ceramics, but research the cost first and determine if that is a material worth investing in.

Decorating

Instead of making your own cauldron from scratch, maybe you wish to decorate or embellish an existing one. Of course, some methods of embellishing really won't be well suited for use with liquids or fire, but if you've already got a "decorative use only" cauldron, there's no harm in blinging it up! You can paint your cauldron, encrust it with jewels, knit a cozy for it—wherever your creativity leads you.

Choosing a Time to Make Your Cauldron

The next thing you may wish to do before constructing your cauldron is to consult a calendar—one with both lunar and solar information. If you have a specific purpose in mind for your cauldron, then you may wish to create it during a time that will help imbue it with those energies. Here are some associations to consider.

Lunar Cycle

New Moon

The dark of the moon is the "seed" stage—imagine a seed waiting to grow within the dark of the earth. This period is ideal for new beginnings, inner contemplation, and scrying. The downside of the new moon is that it's a relatively short period of time in which to get a piece made—only one to two days.

Waxing Moon

The new crescent of the moon is about moving forward and building energy and is ideal for spellcraft that focuses on increasing and encouraging growth. The waxing moon lasts from the first appearance of the new crescent until the moon is full, which gives you a decent amount of time to work on making your cauldron.

Full Moon

The full moon is the time of peak maximum energy of the lunar cycle, and is generally a good all-purpose time to infuse energy into something you have made. Traditionally, the full moon is considered to be about three days long (the length of time it appears to be at maximum fullness to the naked eye), so it's another relatively short time in which to complete your cauldron. If you're casting your cauldron using a lost wax method, consider carving and building during the waxing moon, then cast and hand-finish it during the actual full moon. Similarly, you could build a piece out of clay, allow it to dry, and then fire it at the full moon.

Waning Moon

The waning crescent signifies decreasing energy and is an ideal time for banishing and cleansing work. It can also symbolize preparing for restfulness and healing. You could work on a wax model of your cauldron during the waning moon and cast it during the new moon.

Solar Cycle

Within many Pagan traditions, you will find some variation of the concept of the Wheel of the Year, typically describing eight points of the year: the solstices (summer and winter), the equinoxes (fall and spring), and then the four points in between (Imbolc, Beltane, Lughnasadh, and Samhain are the most common names). Where these all land and flow on the calendar wheel depends on what hemisphere you live in, and the names can and will differ from path to path. Some traditions observe only the equinoxes and solstices, and some have other important days linked to specific historic events and celebrations of deities, so choose what works best for you.

The correspondences I am providing here are meant to give you inspiration. In the end, if you choose to make something from scratch, the most important thing is that you take the time to craft it well, and be mindful of how and why you are making it—regardless of what the sun and moon are doing at the time. In addition to timing considerations for making and/or blessing your cauldron, I've also included activity ideas for using your vessel for each sabbat.

Sabbat Correlations
Imbolc/Candlemas (early February in the Northern Hemisphere)

Aligned with the seed energy of the new moon, Imbolc (meaning "in the belly") is about the promise of the new year. It's typically associated with Brigid, who has metalworking as one of her attributes, so it's a good time to start!

Imbolc Activities: Decorate your cauldron with items sacred to Brigid, inspired by the many things she is considered to be the patroness of. To call upon her medicinal leanings, dry-wash the cauldron with healing dried herbs to make a sachet or start a tincture. To call upon her protection of cattle/sheep/ livestock, decorate the cauldron with images of these animals or products from them that you feel comfortable with (such as wool braids), or bless a cup of milk. For her poetry aspect, inscribe a short poem on the cauldron with chalk. For her sacred well aspect, you can bless water to use for anointing or prepare melted snow (if available) for special uses in the cauldron.

Spring Equinox/Ostara (mid-March in the Northern Hemisphere)

This equinox is a time of balance and the beginning of spring. This is a good time to begin new projects and for workings dealing with increasing/growing energy.

Ostara Activities: You can decorate your cauldron with fertility symbols—reclaiming those bunny rabbits, early spring flowers, and eggs, right? You can also bless seeds in your cauldron before you start planting.

Beltane (May 1 in the Northern Hemisphere)

Beltane is a celebration of fertility, of blessing the land and animals, and a time when the veils between the worlds are considered thin. This is an ideal time for workings involving growth, creativity, inspiration, and prosperity.

Beltane Activities: You can decorate your cauldron with a crown of flowers and wrap it with red and white ribbons—if you don't plan on doing any burning activities. If you do plan on lighting a fire, then traditionally a Beltane fire is used for blessing. You can jump over it or, more safely, light two cauldrons, space them apart in the center of your space, and walk between them. (Mind your clothing, if you have any on!)

Summer Solstice/Litha (mid-June in the Northern Hemisphere)

This solstice is the beginning of summer and the longest day of the year/shortest night. It is ideal for light-focused work, earth-centered workings, and preparation.

Litha Activities: Decorate your cauldron with the flowers and fruits of the early harvest. My favorite suggestion to celebrate the long day is to use your cauldron as a punch bowl and make Midsummer margaritas.

Lughnasadh/Lammas (August 1 in the Northern Hemisphere)

Lughnasadh is the time of the first harvest, a celebration of bounty, and a time for being mindful of the work to come and getting down to business.

Lughnasadh Activities: I always think of bread when I consider this sabbat, so one idea is to make and use a bread bowl as your cauldron/centerpiece, fill it with some tasty goodness, and have everyone partake of it. If you have any leftovers, the crows will be glad to have them. You could also use your cauldron as a fondue pot, and dip into it with freshly baked bread.

Fall Equinox/Mabon (mid-September in the Northern Hemisphere)

This equinox is the start of fall and a time of equal day and night. The focus of this celebration is the main harvest and preparing for winter.

Mabon Activities: This is a great time to set up a beautiful altar reminiscent of a cornucopia, full of items from the harvest. You can make a hearty stew or cider and serve it from the cauldron.

Samhain (October 31/November 1 in the Northern Hemisphere)

The opposite of Beltane, and also considered to be a time when the veils between this world and the next are thin, this celebration honors the dead, ancestors, and spirits. This is an ideal time to bless the cauldron if you plan on doing work with ancestors, the Mighty Dead, spirits, and divination.

Samhain Activities: You can make a special meal (something very aromatic) for departed loved ones or ancestors. With all of the Halloween décor available, you could decorate your cauldron for the spirits or make it a central part of your ancestral altar. Light a spirit candle within the cauldron to honor the dead.

Winter Solstice/Yule (mid-December in the Northern Hemisphere)

This solstice is the start of winter and the longest night/ shortest day. This festival is about finding light in the darkness, finding fulfillment, and celebrating family.

Yule Activities: Brew wassail or a similar beverage in the cauldron. Decorate the cauldron with evergreens and holiday décor. Have everyone bring a small wrapped gift and do a surprise exchange out of the cauldron.

Purchasing Your Own Cauldron

And now…the acquisition! You have several choices in selecting your own cauldron, depending on your needs, preferences, and budget. You could purchase a new one, go on a thrifting or antiquing quest, or rediscover something you already have that might work perfectly. Let's see what may work best for you.

The Shiny New Cauldron

Maybe you're not so inclined to create a cauldron from scratch, and that's totally fine! Despite the fact that cauldrons are not the primary tool for cooking anymore, it's still pretty darn easy to find them and purchase them brand-new. Just because you purchased one versus making it yourself doesn't make it any less special once you've claimed it. Consider the trade-based system of most societies: if you weren't a blacksmith or metalworker, you would exchange your own services to get what you needed—either through bartering directly or by selling your goods to generate money so you could purchase someone else's goods.

So where should you go shopping for your cauldron? The easiest answer is online. There is a multitude of metaphysical shops online, not to mention Etsy, Amazon, eBay, etc. You can read about the various kinds, sizes, makes, and models and compare pricing all online. But alas, you can't touch them, see how they feel in your hands, test the weight, or look over the finish. Convenience does have its price.

If not being able to feel your cauldron before you purchase it is a deal-breaker for you, then luckily there's the good old-fashioned way to purchase one—from a store:

- Most occult, metaphysical, or New Age shops carry cauldrons. To see if there is a store near you, fire up the google machine (using any of the three descriptors I just used, as well as "Pagan," "Witch," or "Wiccan," plus your city, state, etc.), or check out witchvox.com.
- Camping/outdoor supply stores and hardware stores (and the camping supply areas of department and general stores) are good places to look.
- Antique and oddity shops are also good options. While you can certainly find used cauldrons at antique shops,

I've found that many shops also stock brand-new ones, especially in the fall, for both use and decoration.

The Thrifty Cauldron

While buying new is one option, you can also buy a used cauldron. Keep your eyes peeled at thrift stores, antique shops, flea markets, and garage sales. It's important to consider the condition of the cauldron (just how much rust are you *really* willing to clean up?) and the fact that you may not know exactly what kind of material it is made of—which may impact how you use it.

I feel it is important to bring up the saying "Don't bargain/haggle for your magical tools." I don't know who was the first person to start saying that, but I am fairly sure they were trying to sell something. There are many cultures throughout the world where haggling is part of the regular practice of making *any* sort of purchase, and with flea markets and garage sales it's often considered part of the game. So if you see a cauldron you are very much interested in at a flea market but it's slightly out of your price range, don't be afraid to throw a lower price out there—you'll probably get it!

In the spirit of adventure, also don't be afraid to look outside of the cauldron box for similarly-shaped items that may suit your needs. You may find ceramic bowls, brass or bronze vessels, unusual dishes, and other items that may work perfectly for you!

Repurposing: Use What You Have

Maybe you're not in a position to make your own cauldron *or* purchase one. Then it's time to look in your home and see what you have that will work, ideally starting in the kitchen. If you plan on using your cauldron mainly for kitchen witchery, then there's no reason your favorite pot or skillet can't double as your cauldron. If you're looking to do other workings that don't involve edibles, maybe there's a pot or bowl you don't really use. Or maybe a friend or someone in your family just got new cookware or is moving and wants to lighten their load—see if there's anything that will work, and you'll give it new life!

Rethinking the Usual

- Boilers, saucepans, and mixing bowls all make great deep cauldrons (and usually have lids!).
- Old ceramic bowls and dishware are great for mixing, holding, and divination and can be used as ritual markers or candleholders.
- Plates are good for burning candles and incense and setting up altars and can be used as offering plates.

chapter
4

Getting Started

Now that you have your cauldron, let's get started! To begin, we will go over the concepts of cleansing, blessing, and consecrating your cauldron, making it truly your own. We will look at wear, care, and maintenance, including how to season a cast-iron cauldron. We will also think about preparation of the space in which you will use your cauldron to create a proper working environment. Last but not least, we will address important safety issues and healthy practices.

How to Cleanse Your Cauldron

Cleansing your cauldron refers to removing unwanted energies that may be attached to it. Whether you're purchasing a new or used cauldron, it's generally a good idea to cleanse it. I will talk about blessing and consecration next, either of which can be done in the same ritual, if you wish. So be sure to read this whole section before performing your ritual and decide what feels right for you.

Cleansing Ritual

You Will Need: A small bowl of water, sage (smudge stick) and a fireproof dish to rest it in, a small amount of sea salt, a white candle (a tealight is fine), a lighter or matches, and a small towel.

Begin by cleaning the cauldron to make sure it is free of dirt and dust, then thoroughly dry it. Set out the clean cauldron and all of your materials before you.

Ritual: Light the candle and, going counterclockwise (widdershins), pass the candle over and around the cauldron three times, saying, *With the power of fire, I cleanse this cauldron.*

Set the candle down and use it to light the sage, then gently blow it out so it smokes. Circling the smudge stick around the cauldron just like you did with the candle, say, *With the power of air, I cleanse this cauldron.*

Set the smudge stick down on the dish, and pick up the salt. Pour the salt into the cauldron, swishing it around counterclockwise three times, saying, *With the power of earth, I cleanse this cauldron.*

Empty the salt out of the cauldron, making sure it's completely empty. Pick up the water. Pour it into the cauldron, generating a counterclockwise swirl again, saying, *With the power of water, I cleanse this cauldron.*

Empty the water out of the cauldron, and pick up the towel to dry it, saying, *This cauldron has now been cleansed. So mote it be.*

Blow out the candle, snuff out the smudge, and properly dispose of the salt and water. Place the cauldron where you intend to keep it.

Preparing to cleanse your cauldron

Note: You can also add the element of spirit by calling upon a specific deity or deities to help cleanse the cauldron. If you choose to have a physical representation for this additional step, select something that symbolizes that deity or is considered an acceptable offering to them. For example, let's say your patron goddess is Demeter. I would suggest taking a shaft of wheat and moving it around the cauldron counterclockwise, then placing it across the mouth of the vessel, saying, *In the name of Demeter, this cauldron is cleansed.* (If you don't have a shaft of wheat handy, you could also use a sprinkling of flour in the same way that you used the salt.)

Extra Cleansing: Maybe the cauldron you selected seems to have a bit of a funk to it—an energy or attached feeling that you're not happy with. Objects can pick up a sort of spiritual or psychic residue from the people or places they were in contact with. Sometimes that's good and you get good sensations from that object, but sometimes that's bad, especially if the object was around negative emotions or situations.

But luckily, you can "reset" your cauldron to neutral if you need to. I suggest performing the cleansing ritual (just described) on the full moon. Then place the cauldron in a dark pillowcase or wrap it up in thick heavy cloth (like velvet), insulating it. After wrapping it up, place sea salt and hematite in the depression of the mouth area, then tuck the cauldron away in a dark place, close to the earth (like a basement), for at least two weeks (until the new moon). Then pull it out and perform the blessing.

Welcoming a Cauldron

Let's say you have been gifted a cauldron from someone special (a relative, a coven member, a mentor, etc.). What should you do? In this case, you will want to *welcome* the cauldron instead of cleansing it. Welcoming it acknowledges the previous owner's energy and introduces it to your own energy harmoniously.

Welcoming Ritual

You Will Need: Herbs of welcome, a small pouch for the herbs, a white candle, and a lighter or matches.

What are herbs of welcome? These will vary depending on your personal preferences and those of the person you received the cauldron from. For me, rose petals, rosemary, and mugwort would be my top three herbs to use for welcoming. Roses have personal meaning for me and are also generally used as a gift of appreciation and recognition. Rosemary is an herb special to our tradition, and invigorates and blesses. Mugwort is a wonderful herb that has a variety of magical uses. Now let's say the previous owner of the cauldron loved lavender, then that would be a great herb to throw into the mix. Essentially you are bringing a new tool into the family, but giving a nod of recognition to where it came from.

Ritual: Set out the cauldron and your gathered materials. Light the candle, saying, *With the power of fire, symbolic of the hearth, I welcome this cauldron into my home.*

Next sprinkle the herbs into the cauldron, adding one at a time (adjusting the phrasing to suit the herbs and attributions to fit your choices), saying, *I welcome you with lavender in honor of _____. I welcome you with rose petals to recognize the beauty of this gift. I welcome you with mugwort to bless our new relationship. I welcome you with rosemary to invigorate a new practice together.*

Next, swirl the herbs clockwise (deosil) five times, saying, *I thank (name of person) for the gift of this cauldron and welcome it into my home with the blessings of these herbs.*

Funnel the herbs into the pouch and secure it. You may place the pouch inside the cauldron or affix it to the handle so that it keeps its "gift" with it for as long as you like or need. Blow out your candle and place the cauldron in its new home.

Blessing a Cauldron

Once your cauldron has been cleansed, you can bless it, waking it up to your workings and specific divine energies. A blessing can be fairly generic, without indicating a specific purpose. This works especially well if your cauldron is going to be multipurpose. Any object can be blessed, and it's usually done regularly or as needed. Consider the annual "blessing of the fleets," in which fishing boats are blessed for protection, prosperity, and good luck. People often like to call upon the elements or deities to bless items, so I'll give you a few examples.

Elemental Blessing

You Will Need: A small bowl of water, a feather, a small amount of sea salt, a white candle (a tealight is fine), a lighter or matches, and a small towel.

Ritual: Light the candle and, going clockwise, pass the candle over and around the cauldron three times, then place it in the cauldron, saying, *I call upon the element of fire to bless this cauldron. May it be a vessel of warmth and always have a good relationship with fire.*

Remove the candle and set it aside. Pick up the feather, circling the cauldron with it clockwise three times and placing it across the mouth of the cauldron, saying, *I call upon the element of air to bless this cauldron. May it be a vessel of knowledge and bring forth to my workings the breath of inspiration.*

Set the feather aside and pick up the sea salt. Pour the salt into the cauldron, swishing it around clockwise three times, saying, *I call upon the element of earth to bless this cauldron. May it be a vessel of stability and be harmonious with the bounty of the earth.*

Empty the salt out of the cauldron, making sure it's completely empty. Pick up the water and pour it into the cauldron, generating a clockwise swirl again, saying, *I call upon the element* of water to bless this cauldron. May it be a vessel of transformation and at peace with the nature of water.

Empty the water out of the cauldron and pick up the towel to dry it, saying, *This cauldron has been blessed by fire, air, earth, and water. So mote it be.*

Blow out the candle, properly dispose of the salt and water, and put your materials always. Place the cauldron where you intend to keep it.

Deity Blessing Ritual

You can add to the previous elemental blessing a deity or spirit blessing, or do this entirely by itself. I've included three blessings here to give you a sense of how it could be done.

Ceridwen Blessing

Offering: About a tablespoon of dried sandalwood, vervain, or patchouli and a tealight candle.

Ritual: Take three slow deep breaths, then light the candle and place it in the cauldron. Crush some of the herbs with your hands and sprinkle them over the candle, saying, *Hail to Ceridwen, mother, Witch, goddess of inspiration and magick. I call upon you and your wisdom to bless this cauldron. May it be a vessel of knowledge, revelation, and successful workings. May it be blessed in your name.*

Then sprinkle some more crushed herbs. Close your eyes and focus on the deity and the cauldron. You may leave the candle burning if you wish, or, if you are satisfied, gently blow it out and conclude the ritual.

The Dagda Blessing

Offering: Food or drink, such as a small loaf of bread or a mug of beer, and a tealight candle.

Blessing: Take three slow deep breaths, then light the candle and place it on the other side of the cauldron away from you. Pick up your choice of offering and place it in the cauldron, saying, *I call upon the Dagda, the All-Father, the Good One, Lord of the Unending Bounty. Please accept this offering and bless this cauldron. May its workings be fruitful and may all who gather around this cauldron do so in peace and love. So mote it be.*

Close your eyes and focus on the deity and the cauldron. You may leave the candle burning if you wish, or, if you're satisfied, gently blow it out and conclude the ritual by leaving the offering outside for the animals (or pour the beer into the earth).

Hecate Blessing

Offering: A bulb of garlic and a tealight candle. (You can also choose to burn herbs sacred to Hecate, using the Ceridwen blessing as a guideline.)

Blessing: Take three slow deep breaths, then light the candle and place it on the other side of the cauldron away from you. Pick up the garlic bulb and place it in the cauldron, saying,

Great Goddess Hecate, Guardian of the Crossroads, Keeper of the Mysteries, I call upon you to bless this cauldron. May it be a vessel of insight and clarity and a gateway between the worlds. Guide and protect those who work around it, and strengthen the magick made within it. In your name, may this cauldron be blessed!

Close your eyes and focus on the deity and the cauldron. You may leave the candle burning if you wish, or, if you're satisfied, gently blow it out and conclude the ritual by planting the bulb in the earth. You could also incorporate the bulb into a dish and/or leave it outside as an offering.

Stirring the Cauldron:
Consecrating Your Cauldron

A CAULDRON IS a magical tool. To the Celts it was very special, as it represented a place between the worlds—a place of transformation and rebirth. These ancient tribes knew that a most powerful place was where water and fire met. In my practices, this means the cauldron.

On a night when the moon is between phases (exact full or new moon), take a cauldron to the seashore while the tide is coming in. Set the cauldron on the beach just into the damp sand where the highest of waves dampen the earth. This space is neither wet nor dry. Light a fire in the cauldron, which has been prepared for this sacred use (placing only appropriate wood and herbs in the cauldron). From a distance, sit in a comfortable chair set in the sand and watch each successive wave return to the cauldron, slowly surrounding and eventually encompassing it. When the seawater is entirely around the cauldron, then the iron cauldron is between water and fire—in a place left only to the gods, the spirits, and the Mighty Dead. Here your cauldron will charge with power. Watch it until the water has risen to a point where it flows into the cauldron and puts out the fire. Retrieve your cauldron and wash and dry it well. It is now ready for the most powerful of works.

Andrew Theitic
Historian, NECTW Tradition •
Publisher, *The Witches' Almanac* •
Author, *The Witches' Almanac*,
***The Rede of the Wiccae*, and**
A Listing of Botanicals and
***Their Cosmological Attributions* •**
Questions can be directed to
Theitic@nectw.org

The Consecrated Cauldron

If you're designating your cauldron for specific ritual use and you're spiritually inclined, I recommend consecrating it. A blessing can be done to any object, which can then be used for any type of purpose. With consecration, the object acquires a distinctive sacred, otherworldly context. Consecration is essentially the act of taking something from the ordinary world and making it exclusively part of the sacred world. It is typically believed that once something has been consecrated, it is forever changed. So if you're thinking of brewing supper in your cauldron for a party or mixing up a casual pot of tea, but you also want to use the cauldron for brewing sacred mulled wine, then I'd skip consecrating it and just stick with blessing it.

How-To: To consecrate an object, you can add this step onto the cleansing and/or blessing ritual by simply adding in a line about your sacred intent as well as declaring ownership.

Elemental Add-On Sample: This cauldron has been purified and blessed by the element of fire. It is owned by me, (your name), and I claim it for use in my sacred rites. So mote it be.

Deity Add-On Sample: This cauldron has been cleansed and blessed for and by the goddess Hecate. It is owned by us, (coven/group name), and it is claimed for use in our sacred rites, in devotion to and in honor of Hecate. So mote it be.

Attuning Your Cauldron

Attuning means to align an object more closely with your own energy—to put your own mark or energy stamp on it. An item that you make from scratch, carefully adorn, or season naturally becomes attuned to you because of the amount of time and physical contact you have with it. If it's something you didn't make or can't season, then take the time to examine, clean, and run your hands over the cauldron. Give it a gentle bath (if the material allows) and dry it with care. If you have a working altar, that's a great place to keep the cauldron before you start using it. Or you could wrap it in a favorite cloth or piece of clothing and tuck it under the bed near where you rest your head. (I wouldn't recommend sleeping with it under your pillow, because that would be uncomfortable—and silly.)

Care and Feeding of Cauldrons

If you have a decent, well-made cauldron, as long as you treat it well and with respect, it will last a long, long time—remember those Bronze Age cauldrons? This means that every time you use your cauldron, take the time to clean and dry it properly after you are done with your work.

One of the biggest issues with metal is interaction with salt, acids, and water, which can cause rust and other kinds of corrosion. In particular, salts and acids are the biggest antagonists of metals. Their actions can be accelerated when different types of metal come in contact with each other in addition to the presence of water. For example, leaving a copper spoon in an iron cauldron essentially makes a battery and will lead to rapid corrosion. So if you're using a different kind of metal to stir your cauldron than the one it's made of, don't leave the utensil in there for prolonged periods of time, or use something non-reactive instead, like wood, glass, or plastic, to stir or ladle.

Don't store food or liquid in your cauldron either, unless it's specifically designed for it. If you're cooking or brewing in your cauldron, once it's done, transfer your food or brew to a proper storage container. If you want to use your cauldron as a decorative food container, find a smaller bowl that fits inside of it or sits nicely just over the lip, and put your food in that instead. That will create much less hassle and be far easier to clean up than having a salt- or acid-loaded food or drink sitting in your cauldron for hours.

After a long ritual or working, it's very tempting to just let it all go and worry about the mess in the morning. Not only could this lead to potential damage and a *lot* more work, but you're also not being very respectful of the actions and tools you just put your energy into. If you're working outside and leave the mess for later, you may be in for a lot more work in no time at all thanks to the elements—especially if you live near salt water. Trust me, you'll be glad you took the extra five to ten minutes to clean up!

How you clean your cauldron depends on what you've done with it and what kind of cauldron it is. If you've just been using herbs and water, then you should be able to simply give it a warm rinse and dry it completely. If you've been using oils, salts, and sticky things, you'll want to do a light soapy hand scrub, then rinse and pat dry. If you've made a waxy mess of your cauldron from loose candles, there are a few things you can do. Sometimes it's easier to clean out wax once it cools, and it may just peel off. If that doesn't work, warm up the cauldron until the wax melts and pour as much of it out as possible. Use newsprint to wipe up the rest. This may take several attempts until it's completely clean. (For more tips on cleaning seasoned cast-iron cauldrons, please see the next section.)

Once your cauldron and other tools are clean and *thoroughly dry*, it's time to put them back in their homes—and don't mix materials if you can help it. If an item is out in the open on a special shelf or bookcase, be sure to dust it and give it some love when it's not in use. Some people keep their cauldrons on or near their altars, while others have a special closet, cabinet, or box where they store their magical tools. Putting your cauldron somewhere safe and secure grants peace of mind. Otherwise you never know when an unsuspecting partner or roommate who is desperately looking for a container to catch water from a roof leak might grab your favorite pot and make short use of it. (Yes, I speak from experience!)

Seasoning Your Cast-Iron Cauldron

You've probably heard the term *seasoning* but aren't sure what it is, how to do it, or if you even should. Seasoning refers to the coating produced when a layer of animal or vegetable fat is applied to and cooked onto cast-iron cookware. This layer causes the surface to be stick-resistant and tends to improve with added use and care. Some cauldrons come "pre-seasoned," which means the coating has already been applied. If you don't have one of those, then you'll want to follow these directions to season your cast-iron cauldron.

If you have a non-seasoned cauldron, start by giving it a hot, soapy bath with a good scrubbing to remove any oils from the manufacturing/casting process. Then dry your cauldron completely so there is no water left on or in it. Using the oil of your choice, thoroughly coat your cauldron inside and out with the aid of a cloth or paper towel, then wipe off any excess oil. You may want to place the cauldron upside down over a newspaper for about an hour to drain off any extra oil. Line the bottom of your oven with aluminum foil to catch any more drops, and preheat your oven to 350°F. Place the cauldron upside down on the center rack and let it bake for thirty minutes. Turn off the oven and let the cauldron cool. Now it's ready!

Do *not* treat your seasoned cauldron like ordinary cookware by scouring it or putting it in the dishwasher, or you will discover a world of hurt (and rust). Hardcore cast iron fans recommend just wiping out the pan after use, or washing it with warm water and a stiff brush (not wire!) if there's a lot of food residue. The more you cook with your seasoned vessel, the more likely the coating will continue to build up slowly. Others suggest scrubbing the pot with coarse salt and a paper towel or rag to clean it. If you still wish to use soap, choose something very mild and hand-wash the pan, dry it, and then reapply a thin layer of fat or oil. Also, if you cook acidic foods often (such as tomato sauce), this will remove the seasoning in your pan fairly quickly, so you'll need to re-season the pan from time to time.

When Tragedy Befalls Your Cast-Iron Cauldron

Oops, you knew better, but you did it anyway, and now your cauldron is rusty. Or maybe you just found a lovely old cauldron that needs some TLC. What can you do about it? Here are some options.

The Elbow Grease Method

As you may have guessed, this method involves physically scouring off the rust in the pan, either with steel wool, sandpaper, or a motor tool with a steel brush attachment (being careful not to work on any one spot for too long). This is the quickest way when you just have some light rust to remove. Then clean and season your cauldron.

Health Tip: Wear gloves and work in a well-ventilated area. I also recommend wearing a surgical mask or at least covering your nose and mouth with a cotton bandana or scarf to avoid inhaling rust particles.

Incinerate

For more severe rust and buildup, there is the old-school method of tossing the cauldron into a bonfire or fireplace for several hours. The fire will strip the cast iron of seasoning and turn the rust to ash. If you don't have access to a fire but have a self-cleaning oven, several people I know swear by the method of simply placing the cauldron inside the oven on the self-cleaning cycle. But this method takes a lot of energy and could potentially damage your oven, so caution is recommended. After some light scrubbing, your cauldron should be ready for a fresh coat of seasoning.

Additional Cleaning Methods

There are also chemical options for cleaning your pan, such as commercial brands designed to remove rust, usually made with lye or vinegar. But they take even more time and babysitting, plus you *must* work in a well-ventilated area. A somewhat safer and more effective cleaning option is electrolysis—using an electrical current and mild basic solution to lift away the rust. Several of my Steampunk/maker friends swear by this method, though I suspect it has to do largely with them feeling a bit like mad scientists when they do it. If you have a badly rusted piece and this sounds intriguing to you, then a quick search online will lead you to a multitude of free instructional videos and how-tos.

The Working Space Around Your Cauldron

Some people spend a lot of time and money on their magical tools but neglect to pay any attention to the space where they are working. I am all for making magick when and where you can, if there's an immediate need, but I find I get much better results when I take the time to prepare the space. Preparation always starts with elbow grease—meaning a good physical cleaning and tidying up. Consider this: It's rather hard to think about doing an emotional cleansing and regeneration in your bathtub when it's covered in soap scum and mildew.

Likewise, it's difficult to cook a magical meal of celebration when your kitchen is filthy and you can't find anything.

While it may seem rather mundane, there is much to be said for physically cleaning and organizing the space you work in. When I'm feeling angry, depressed, or out of sorts, I find great satisfaction in making sure my home is in order, even if it's just one room. It truly is a form of sympathetic magick—by cleaning and tidying up your living space, you'll feel the energy in your space improve as well. You are effectively making a physical impact on your environment, which makes you feel more in control. This sense of control in turn empowers you and helps you focus. Even just a half hour of cleaning that involves light dusting, sweeping, and wiping down surfaces can yield powerful results.

Cauldron Safety: Brewing Danger

I believe it to be of the utmost importance to think about safety when working with cauldrons, cauldron magick, and especially fire. Here are some very important things to be aware of before you start using your cauldron.

Surface

When working with fire, be sure to place your cauldron on a sturdy, fireproof surface—tile, stone, or brick are ideal. You can also line a pan or cooking tray with aluminum foil and place your cauldron on top of that. If you visit a flooring or hardware store that carries stone tile, you can purchase a single large, nice-looking tile to place your cauldron on for fairly cheap.

Ventilation

Always use proper ventilation when burning or boiling. Just because something appears to be smokeless doesn't mean there isn't a harmful gas or vapor being produced. If working inside, work near an open window or with kitchen (or bathroom) vents running. If that isn't possible, consider working outside or using another method. You don't want to pass out because of vapors, smoke, or a lack of air.

Contain Your Candle

If you're placing a candle inside a cauldron, be sure to put the candle in a proper-size container first. Cauldrons are very good at retaining heat, and if your candle liquefies outside of a holder, the melted wax could indeed catch fire and cause quite a mess. Long ago, my open-path group held a public Samhain ritual, and someone brought a hibachi grill to use instead of the smaller cauldron we normally used. A fire was lit inside of it for attendees to use to burn their written intentions. Someone placed a candle inside the grill as well, which melted and started to drip down through the grill opening—catching on fire. The then-liquid fire dripped down to the table (and tablecloth) it was on, which also caught on fire. *Lessons learned:*

don't place uncontained candles in the fire, don't place fires on top of wooden tables, and be wary of chanting the "Samhain Fire Song" with the chorus of "Burn, fire, burn!" with too much gusto.

Put a lid on it

"Natural" Is Not Necessarily Safe

Just because something is "natural" doesn't mean it's safe—for eating, burning, or drinking. There are plenty of herbs that can cause allergic reactions—or worse—when burned. Nor are all parts of the same plant safe to use. Do your research before you use *any* kind of plant part in your cauldron, and always start small and be patient when adding ingredients.

Lid It

If you're burning anything inside your cauldron, *before* you set anything aflame, have the lid handy just in case things get out of hand. A lot can happen in a few precious seconds, so take the time to prepare your working area properly before starting, which includes having the lid in easy reach. If you don't have a proper lid for your cauldron, then find a fireproof object that's larger than the opening of your cauldron and will create a seal that will snuff out the fire.

From Use to Use

If you're using your cauldron for multiple uses (burning, boiling, serving food, etc.), be extra careful about what you prepare in your cauldron to avoid inadvertent poisoning. If you're unsure about possible interactions, then you may want to designate specific vessels for certain uses *only*.

Outside Safety

One obvious benefit of working outside is more ventilation, and it's great to work outside when your inside working space is too warm or small to work in comfortably. But there's a whole new set of things to think about when you move outdoors. If working with fire, make sure the ground and the *sky* are clear around you. I have known folks who have inadvertently set bushes and trees on fire that were overhanging the work area. Work away from vehicles and buildings and check your local laws. Some areas have specific laws about how far a fire can be from a building, as well as what you can burn and when you can do it. There's also the weather: wind, rain, and sudden storms all pose potential problems. Lastly, consider your neighbors. If you can see your neighbor's yard, then they can see yours. Dancing skyclad around your cauldron and bonfire on the full moon is definitely going to give them an eyeful, and possibly give the cops an engraved invitation to visit.

Animals and Offspring

Every seasoned practitioner I know has at least one pet story involving ritual or spellcraft. Cats tend to be very perceptive about wandering in and out of sacred space, whereas dogs tend to be oblivious—but I've also heard the exact opposite! Be mindful of tails, paws, and whiskers getting into whatever you're working on. Children are a whole other matter and often seem to take precautions and warnings as a personal challenge. If there isn't another responsible person available to supervise a child while you're doing a working, then consider finding a way to get them involved in the work so they can "help." One idea that some folks have found helpful is setting a child up with a miniature cauldron and all of the fixings (safe, of course) so they can be just like their parents.

Melting Metal and Other Hazards

It's important to be aware of fusible alloys—that is, a metal alloy capable of being melted easily at relatively low temperatures, generally below 183°C (361°F). This includes combined metals involving tin, lead, bismuth, cadmium, zinc, etc. Unless you know for sure the origin and metallurgy of your cauldron, I recommend exercising caution when applying heat to it (from the outside *or* inside). Many "cauldrons" are made explicitly for decorative purposes, and if they're manufactured in China, India, etc., there's even more reason to be cautious. Having worked in the fashion jewelry industry, I know that dealing with lead and nickel content was a huge issue when importing anything with metal components from those countries. When items are not made to meet specific standards and guidelines, dangerous metals may be used, because they are far less expensive. Hence, if something you purchased says "for decorative purposes only," it's best to be careful in how you use it. Also, some items may be painted to look like cast iron but could be another metal that was simply plated or painted black. Don't set fire directly in it, and don't eat or drink out of it!

Stirring the Cauldron:
The Cauldron as Burning Pot

HAVE YOU EVER thought about using your cauldron for meditation and cleansing/purification?

I use my cauldron as an aid to meditation, to prepare myself for ritual or spellwork, and to cleanse or purify my home or individuals in the room. I was first introduced to the idea of the cauldron as a cleansing tool when attending a meditation group twenty years ago. They would pour a portion of Epsom salts (table salt can be substituted) into the bottom of the vessel and then add grain alcohol or rubbing alcohol. After instructing attendees to focus all their stress, negativity, and other unwanted energies into the flames in the cauldron, they would strike a match or use a long-handled lighter to ignite the alcohol.

Not only does this method produce a neat effect—dancing flames that can range in color from blue to green, depending on the salt—but it also works rather well as a focal point for preparing yourself for meditation. As you stare into the flames, focusing your negative energies into them, you can feel yourself becoming more relaxed and attuned to the task that is before you. You can use this simple meditation technique to prepare for spell or ritual work or simply use it as a meditation.

When you use salts and alcohol for a burning pot, you should clean your cauldron as soon as possible. Don't try to clean it immediately after the flame goes out, since the metal will be hot. I know that's obvious, but you'd be surprised. You can pour room-temperature water into the cauldron after the flames go out to keep the salt soft. The heat of the flames can cause the salt to solidify into a mass. Pouring cold water into the hot cauldron could cause it to crack. If you use the water method, you can dump the contents of the cooled cauldron into a trash can and wipe the residue out of the cauldron. If you choose not to use the water, you may have to gently break up the salt to get it to release. Whichever method you use, you will want to rinse and dry the cauldron thoroughly after cleaning it.

Rev. Philipp J. Kessler
Co-founder and Nebraska Facilitator of the Pagan Alliance Network • Program director and content manager for the Pagan-Musings Podcast Channel, www.PMPChannel.com

In the Circle—Ritual Arts

Of all of the Witch's tools, the cauldron is one of the most versatile, easily traversing the line between mundane applications and metaphysical work. In this chapter we'll explore many of the ways you can use your cauldron for what I call the ritual arts.

What Is Ritual?

Ritual is an often misunderstood entity. When most people think of ritual, they picture a very intricate, ornate, long, or intense ceremony, but it can also be something very simple that you do every day. Ritual can help to bring meaning, pattern, and order to daily life. Rituals have been created to celebrate the seasons, to honor life cycles and transitions (such as birth, coming of age, marriage, eldering, death, etc.), to perform divination, to honor the ancestors, to celebrate community and recognize achievements, and so forth. Ritual can be very elaborate or very simple, as long as it works for you.

Casting a circle

The following quote, from chapter 4 of John K. Nelson's *A Year in the Life of a Shinto Shrine*, is one of my favorite explanations of ritual:

> *It is believed that the human need for some kind of formal, often public acknowledgment of significant events is one of the fundamental forces of our development as social beings. At the same time, ritual allows us to transcend our individual selves to gain a sense of participation with the greater environment of the forces controlling our singular and communal destinies.*

The Cauldron's Place in Ritual

The cauldron has a multitude of uses for ritual. It can be an altar unto itself, be used to mark the quarters or represent the elements, be a point of consecration, invocation, or blessing, or be the focus of a ritual working. For this section, I am focusing on ritual work that involves utilizing cauldrons in ways that don't explicitly involve spellcraft. You can of course include spellcraft within a ritual, and I've included some ideas, but that subject has a chapter all its own.

> *The cauldron involves the powers of the four elements, because it needs water to fill it, fire to heat it, the green herbs or other products of earth to cook in it, while the steam arises from it and spreads its aroma into the air.*
> —Doreen Valiente, *Witchcraft for Tomorrow*, pp. 83–84

The Cauldron as an Altar

Doreen Valiente's quote is a beautifully poetic way of looking at a cauldron as an all-in-one altar. Since it can interact with all of the traditional elements, the cauldron can embody them while taking on other meanings as well, making it a very effective altar.

When you see or hear the word *altar*, you may imagine an elaborate display of statues, offerings, ritual implements, and so forth. There are certainly many altars that fit that description perfectly, in a huge variety of faiths—Catholics, Hindus, Jews, and Pagans alike all make use of altars. But an altar doesn't have to be fancy or take up a lot of space for it to be effective.

What Is an Altar Anyway?

An altar is a designated or special point of focus. It is a place of meditation, for observance, remembrance, and honoring, somewhere to make offerings and sacrifice, a gateway for communicating to the Other and doing other spiritual work. It can be devoted to a specific deity or many gods, to ancestors and other spirits or to the individual practitioner. It can be a permanent installation or temporarily set up for something specific. It can be static and specific to a certain place or it can be mobile.

When the cauldron is used for divination, it can be a place of meditation, focus, and otherworldy connections. When you work a spell within it, it becomes a place of transformation. When you use it as a ritual marker for element, deity, or spirit, it becomes a place of honor, offering, and communication. When you make a special brew, potion, or meal inside of it, it becomes a sacred vessel that contains your work until you're ready to dispense it. It can reside in a special spot where you always use it, or travel with you indoors and out. You could adorn it for sabbats and other special days, filling it with symbolic items such as a magical flower arrangement, or it can be your tabernacle, where you stow away important items and tools when you don't want them to be seen. All of these uses speak to the power of the cauldron as an altar.

How-To: As you can see from the previous description, it's rather easy to make the cauldron your altar. It's how you maintain it that really makes the difference.

Consecrating Your Cauldron

After cleaning, cleansing, and blessing your cauldron, it's ready to be used in any working. If you have a specific rite or use, then you can perform an additional consecration for that purpose. Here are some examples of consecrations.

Seer's Cauldron

In preparation for divination, I call upon the Fates to bless this cauldron. May it be a worthy vessel and aid me in seeing the patterns and threads that you weave with clarity, insight, and understanding.

As you say this, you can wrap a thread around the lip of the cauldron or anywhere else where it won't be an obstruction or fire hazard when you use it. The thread is in honor of the Fates.

Brewing Cauldron

Within the walls of this cauldron, I will stir and make a mighty brew. May the gods bless this vessel and the fruits of my work. So mote it be.

Tap the lip of the cauldron three times with a wand, athame, or instrument of brewing, then begin your work.

Communication Altar

May this cauldron be the gateway between the divine and myself. May it and the workings within it and around it be protected, safe, and made sacred.

As you say this, wave your hand (or athame or wand) over and around the cauldron three times in a counterclockwise motion.

Ancestral Altar

I consecrate this cauldron in honor of my grandmother, (grandmother's name). May the kindness, wisdom, and wit she shared with me in her kitchen and throughout life be a guide and an inspiration. May the meals I cook within it do her memory honor and nourish us physically, mentally, and spiritually. Blessed be.

If you have a small pin, charm, ribbon, or other item reminiscent of your ancestor that you can affix to the cauldron, do so as you say this blessing.

After you're finished using your cauldron as an altar, clean it properly, cleanse it if necessary, and place it back where it belongs.

Folklore: Gateway to the Gods

For a long time, the hearth was considered the heart of the home, and there is much folklore surrounding it from a great many cultures throughout history. The hearth was the center of life—where food was made and feasts were enjoyed and where stories and myths were shared, oaths were sworn, pacts were made, and rites were enacted. It was truly a place of many purposes and of magick, often with the cauldron at the center of it all.

In Slavic and similar Eastern European traditions, there is much importance placed upon the *verige*—the chain that holds the cauldron above the fire and connects it to the chimney. As the chain exists in an in-between place—between the earth and the sky, yet not quite touching either—it is considered to be a direct link to deities and other worlds. How it is treated and decorated can have much influence over the well-being of the household, so it is well taken care of. By direct association with the verige, the cauldron becomes a sacred place as well. (For more information, I recommend *Balkan Traditional Witchcraft* by Radomir Ristic.)

Ritual Markers

Many practitioners create sacred space in which to work by casting a circle or similar consecration of space for a limited time. How this is done varies from tradition to tradition, path to path, and person to person. While some people are lucky enough to have a special room for their practice, or are part of a congregation that has their own church, temple, or sacred circle, most of us make do with creating temporary spaces in our homes, yards, woods, etc. A benefit of casting a circle is that you can do it anywhere, at any time, and leave no evidence of your work. This comes in handy when you live or work in an area where public knowledge of your practices may put you in jeopardy.

One way to make your temporary space feel and look more "real" is to set up markers for the quarters and/or elements. Most commonly you will find the four cardinal directions assigned for the quarters (north, east, south, and west), and sometimes the concept of above and below. The elements are often defined as earth, air, fire, and water—and, in quite a few traditions, spirit as well. Asian (particularly Chinese) traditions will have Wood, Fire, Earth, Metal, and Water. The more formal and rooted in ceremonial magick a tradition is, the more elaborate and complex the markers become. Some traditions are very simple in their procedure and may invoke specific spirits or landforms that are central to their practice.

Confused yet? One more detail: which quarters and elements are associated with each other will differ as well—if they call upon both or any at all. So how many and which ones *you* choose depends on your own beliefs and practices.

Marking the directions

I think it's best to start with *why* you would choose to acknowledge the directions or elements. The quarters effectively mark the boundaries of the space you are working in, defining and protecting the space you work in from the outside world. Elementals, spirits, and deities are called in to watch over the proceedings, lend their energy, and protect the circle and those within it. It's essentially inviting over some good neighbors, treating them with hospitality, and getting a good party out of it for everyone.

My job here is give you some ideas of how to incorporate cauldrons as markers in your ritual practice, so use them as guidelines to inspire you, and consider your RSVP list thoughtfully. We'll look at creating markers by direction, elements, land (genius loci), and divine energy.

Wait, How Many Cauldrons Am I Going to Need for This?

You will need as many markers as you wish to call upon—however, I'm not expecting everyone to run out and purchase five matching cauldrons. I am rather partial to the number five, as it's considered a sacred number, representing the hand, blessing, protection, action, and cycles. I was lucky that my first (and still favorite) cauldron happened to come along with a large bowl that sits inside of it, plus four smaller matching bowls, so that was mighty convenient! I expect most practitioners will want something small and practical. For this exercise, the term *cauldron* can mean a bowl or a deep dish, a votive holder, or any sort of container. From a "dipping" bowl (for condiments) to teacups and soup bowls, you have a variety of options you can find or purchase inexpensively. If you have the budget and you'd really like to have a set of identical cauldrons, then go for it, but it's not necessary.

Marking the Directions: The Space Around Us

The cardinal points give us a sense of not only where we are at but also where we are going and where we have come from. And when we follow them continuously from north to south until we head north again, and from west to east until we are in the west again, we create a sphere. The center of the sphere pinpoints where you are physically. If you can visualize the cardinal directions heading out horizontally away from you, you may also be inclined to consider the metaphysical idea of "As above, so below," which references our connection with the divine, the spirits, ancestors, etc. So by having physical markers to designate the directions in your space, they can help you keep this in mind as you work within the space.

How-To: This kind of marker is very simple, though you can definitely get more elaborate with it if you wish. You can write or paint the name or initial of the direction directly on the vessel, or you can use a fireproof material (many ribbons sold commercially today have been treated to resist fire) to make a banner or sash for it. Color coordination can be achieved by researching what your area's or culture's colors are for the directions, as this can vary greatly. If you are unsure, create a sash using a wide white or cream ribbon, and write on it with a black marker. Using a black ribbon and a metallic marker is another option. You could also fill the vessel with sand, salt, or dirt, and draw the initial into the sediment—or make the initial out of the material itself, though that takes more work. The sash and fill methods are ideal for vessels that have multiple uses, because you're not permanently marking the container.

From there you can place a tealight candle in the vessel. (A real candle is good, but a battery-operated one won't set curious cats or children on fire.) Use a compass (or the GPS on your phone) to determine where north is, and set your markers accordingly.

Note: Marking only the directions and not relating them to elements is a very valid way to mark your space if you're not comfortable with that concept. We all can use some direction at least!

Tip: As you designate a vessel for a specific marker, focus your intention on it, visualizing it. If you wish to say something aloud, here is an idea: *I bless this vessel as a marker of* _____.

Evoking the Elements

To *evoke* means to call upon, draw forth, or produce. I like to describe evoking as welcoming into your space an equal energy—that is, energy that is akin to or part of you. People in many cultures believe we are made up of four or more elements, so they are part of us and the world around us.

You can relate the directions to specific elements, which does make their placement in the space easier. The correspondences I use are north/earth, east/air, fire/south, west/water, and above-below/spirit. Your own correlations may vary depending on your background. If you really think about it, the elements exist in all of the directions, so marking them is really a symbolic gesture, designed to draw attention to each element one at a time, more than anything else. Working with the elements helps us consider the materials and energies that make up the universe, including ourselves and the materials we work with.

How-To: There are many fun ways to combine cauldrons and elements. You can associate certain colors with the elements, or use materials that represent them. The color associations I use are as follows:

Earth: Browns and greens

Air: Light yellow or light purple

Fire: Reds and oranges

Water: All shades of blue

Spirit: White, gold, or silver

You have the option of choosing a container that is already those colors or painting your vessel. Or, for a less permanent solution, you could tie a colored sash/ribbon on your cauldron or fill it with colored sands or salts to align it with a specific element. If you're into collecting (Wunderkammer style), you could fill your container with items that remind you of those elements—or pictures of them.

Here are some suggestions.

Earth: Rocks, soil, dried or living plants and plant material, antler and bones, animals of the land.

Air: Feathers are an obvious one for this element, but be sure to research which feathers you can collect or purchase and possess legally. Other ideas include clear or smoky crystals, items that generate smoke (incense), flying insects, and other animals of the air (wings and things).

Fire: Lava rock, coals, candles, animals of fire or of a fiery nature, tools for making fire.

Water: Water, clean liquid, fish scales or bones, shells, and items from the pond, river, lake, or ocean; animals of the sea (again, please check to make sure you can legally possess the item and aren't impacting the environment before collecting it).

Spirit: Crystal, images of deity.

You can create arrangements in each container (which is also a wonderful way to meditate and commune with the elements), then place them in their corresponding spot in your space. Or, if you simply just want to have or use one cauldron or container, you can place all of the items in it carefully, making it the ultimate altar. Easy!

Note: If you plan on reusing the ingredients in the arrangements, be sure to keep them clean (free from dust) and take care of them.

Elemental Considerations

You can also identify with the elements by acknowledging their elemental spirit forms, which some people find more helpful because it gives a "face" to each element. Though the following entities may sound fantastical, you definitely want to interact with them as respectfully as possible.

Earth Elementals: Gnomes—beings of earth, residing in caves, forests, and groves, many of which are associated with folklore and mythology: plant and tree spirits (dryads and sprites), elven folk, satyrs, brownies, etc.

Water Elementals: Undines—beings of water, living in ponds, lakes, rivers, streams, waterfalls, oceans, marshes and wetlands, fountains, storms, etc. Mermaids, sirens, kelpies, selkies, sea monsters, and water sprites are just a few of the undines.

Fire Elementals: Salamanders—beings of fire, creatures of smoke and flame, such as dragons, snakes, lizards, and other reptilian creatures.

Air Elementals: Sylphs—beings of air, ruling clouds, gases, and the winds, including the Fey (fairies), angels, and other winged creatures.

How-To: You could use images of the elementals to decorate your vessels—a google image search of any of these creatures will lead you to a wealth of images to print out. You could glue them to the front of a glass candleholder, or laminate them, punch holes in the corners, and make a "necklace" for the vessel. Or, using your elemental arrangement when you cast your circle, visualize each elemental and welcome them at each location using the following structure: *Sylphs, beings of air, I welcome you to this sacred space.* Change the name and element as you go, of course. When you have completed your work, thank them and finish with this structure: *Gnomes, beings of earth, I thank you for your presence and bid you farewell.*

Lastly, whether you consider the elements to be metaphors, symbols, physical evidence, or entities, *be respectful.* You don't have to believe in undines to understand that water gives life, but you can also drown in it with very little effort. Fire warms us, but it can also burn us, and smoke suffocates. Breath maintains life, but a tornado can demolish a town.

Earth nourishes us, but the ground still shifts beneath our feet. I'm not saying to be scared of these things, but rather to be mindful in order to have the best interactions and results.

Aligning with the Land and Genius Loci

Some paths and traditions are very much tied to the land. This tenet can present a difficult challenge if your tradition is linked to a land far away from the one in which you reside, hence the rise of bioregional awareness and animism in modern-day Paganism—discovering the sacred where you live. It's rather invigorating *and* sensible to find that connection where you live. Consider your local landscape, both natural and humanmade landmarks. You may find it helpful to also consider their alignment with the cardinal directions (just a suggestion, but not absolutely necessary).

For example, when I lived on the very tip of the peninsula of New Jersey, there was the Delaware River to my west, the Atlantic Ocean to my east, the Pine Barrens National Forest to my north, and the Cape May Beach to my south. Therefore, I could collect samples of water from the river and the ocean to mark my west and east, a sample of sand from the beach for the south, and some pine needles from the forest for north. It does take some time to collect such items, but there are so many benefits to doing this—reconnecting with your surroundings and the spirit of the places, and being able to see how things change as the seasons go by. If you live in a city, don't despair—the sacred is still all around you. In every city in which I have ever lived, there's always been one particular building that I associate with being the heart of the city. A picture of the building or a pebble or plant piece from the grounds can represent that building for you. Is there a certain animal, plant, or natural formation that your city is known for? How about a ticket from the subway to represent south? If you can find a connection, it will have power and meaning for you.

If you're *not* local to the land that's key to your practice, then you can use photos or pictures of landmarks to bring it closer to you. If you're able to travel there on occasion, you could collect actual samples (a rock, a soil or water sample, a pressed and dried flower or leaf from the site, etc.) and use them in your markers, preserved in vials and placed in or near your cauldron.

Invoking Deities and Spirits

Slightly different from evoking is the action of invoking. Invocation involves pulling in the energy from a higher aspect of ourselves, of deities, ancestors, and other divine aspects. Sometimes it can mean literally bringing that energy *inside* of you, but here we're talking about bringing those entities *into* your space. If the elements are your friends whom you are inviting to the party, then deities and spirits are the VIP special guests—who also happen to be the kind of guests who lend their energy to making the party awesome.

We tend to call upon deity particularly when we need some additional help or we give them special focus and honor in our work.

If a tradition uses particular entities, spirits, or gods to mark the quarters, they typically have some sort of sculpture, statue, or banner to represent them. But that can mean a significant investment in money and having somewhere safe to stow them. If you're short on funds or space, turn to the cauldron to represent them instead. To use a cauldron, you can gather items that are sacred to that spirit or deity within the cauldron, making it a miniature altar to them. Or if that spirit or deity has a particular symbol, you could inscribe or paint it on the vessel. Similarly, you could ask deceased loved ones, ancestors, and the Mighty Dead to watch over your work. Using photos or images that remind you of them, or collecting in the cauldron symbols, artifacts, and other items that honor them, are excellent ways to connect with them.

At the end of your work, take the time to thank each of them in turn by name, and bid them farewell.

The Cauldron as a Working Focal Point

When working with a group, the cauldron can be a wonderful focus for a rite—whether it's the altar itself or an integral tool. The cauldron can be used in ritual in the following ways:

- *As a container* for wine (or another appropriate beverage) that will be blessed during the rite and then distributed to the attendees in celebration or observance.
- *As a collection place* for written intentions: for workings where everyone writes down on paper an intent (the name of someone who needs healing, something they wish to bring into their life or banish, a goal, etc.). The intentions may be collected and saved for later, burned in the cauldron to release them, or buried afterward so that they may take root.
- *As a transformer:* Attendees are each asked to focus on a small glass of water in front of them with a message to the ancestors or deities. One by one, they each pour their water into the cauldron, and it is heated up with herbs of blessing, evaporating up to the spirits.
- *As a purifier:* Similar method to the previous one, except that attendees are instructed to focus on something they wish to remove from their life. One by one, they each pour their water into the cauldron, and it is heated up with salt and herbs of cleansing, evaporating away. The cauldron is then cooled, cleaned, and cleansed (or a second cauldron is used instead). New fresh water is brought in and blessed to bring in good energy, and each attendee scoops some into their cup and drinks of it.

- *As a maker:* In the tradition of "stone soup," the cauldron is prepared to make an edible soup or stew. Each person brings a prepared ingredient to the cauldron, and adds it to the brew with a good intention. When the soup is ready, everyone shares it.
- *For oracular divination:* A group may make a special incense blend to burn or perhaps brew a tea with heady steam, then take turns sitting (or designate a specific person to sit) in front of the cauldron as the oracle. Questions are asked and answers recorded.

Jumping the Cauldron

In some traditions, a lit cauldron is jumped over during specific rituals, including initiation, handfasting, purification, and fertility blessing. For initiation, it is meant to represent an ordeal or trial—think back to the mythic "boiling cauldrons." Similarly, it can be done by the wedding couple as part of a handfasting ritual to represent the power of the oath they are making to each other and the bond they are building. Jumping over the cauldron for purification speaks of the cleansing power of fire. Lastly, the fertility blessing harkens back to the sacred bonfires of old—particularly at Beltane when animals would be driven between bonfires to bless them with good health and fertility, and daring individuals and couples may leap over the bonfire as well for the same reason.

Note: Most traditions that jump the cauldron regularly tend to work skyclad—which means there are no cloaks or dresses to catch fire. If you're working with clothes on and you really want to do this, use a candle or small fire, not something you'd roast meat over, and be careful not to wear easily flammable materials and long, loose garments. Also make sure there's plenty of clearance and solid ground around the cauldron to move. You should be in decent health and relatively sober. Have a fire extinguisher or similar safety device handy just in case.

The Cauldron as Part of the Great Rite

I have put this option separately because it is a bit complicated in practice and symbolism.

In Wiccan ritual, the cauldron may be used (instead of a chalice) to represent the Goddess and stand in for the high priestess during a symbolic enactment of what is known as the Great Rite. More traditionally, the Great Rite is the sexual union of the high priest and high priestess to invoke the God and Goddess, but it's more commonly enacted today symbolically (especially for public rites!), using the chalice (held by the high priest) to represent the Goddess and the athame (held by the high priestess) to represent the God. (See Jason Mankey's book *The Witch's Athame*.) Both versions symbolize creation in the fertile union of the Goddess and her God.

As more practitioners of various sexual orientations and non-binary gender identity become prominent in Wicca and similar paths that use this ritual, the place of the Great Rite comes into question for its meaning and effectiveness. Also considering how it appeared and was developed in Gardnerian, Alexandrian, and other offshoot traditions of Wicca, I don't think it was meant to be a standard, catch-all sort of procedure performed at every ritual, yet it has become iconic (not unlike the rite of transubstantiation of the Eucharist in the Catholic Church).

The Great Rite was embraced as a revolutionary ritual by those coming out of the sexually suppressed Victorian era. It brought the sense of the sacred back to the human body, versus looking at the physical self as a vessel of sin. The ritual can be a celebration of sexual union, but for most of the last century in many traditions it was rooted in heterosexual concepts: designated as an act between priestess and priest, a woman and a man. Such a view leaves LGBTQ practitioners (those who identify outside the gender binary and heteronormativity) out in the cold. I think it's important to recognize that sexual release can be a very powerful means of making magick, but it's not exclusive to heterosexual relationships, nor is male-female fertility the root of all magick in any way for many paths. It's really a lot to consider, and this rite's meaning should reside within the practitioner who feels comfortable using it.

That's a long way of saying, if you want to dip your athame into your cauldron to represent sexual union (of the gods, of animals, etc.) because that has personal significance and symbolism for you, then do it. If it doesn't make sense for you, there are plenty of other uses for your cauldron.

Stirring the Cauldron:
A Samhain Rite

I HAVE BEEN a Traditional Witch for many years. I learned the Craft in my youth in the South of England, where the cauldron has always been an integral part of the Craft I still practice today. It is one of the most useful tools I have, and to say that we still use it in our coven rituals today would be an understatement. It is still one of the most integral parts of some, if not all, of our rites.

One of my personal favorites is our Samhain rite, when our coveners and initiates are invited to write a list of any or all of their fears and regrets. This can be quite a long list for those who have not celebrated with us before. During the rite, once we have crossed the veil, they burn their lists in the cauldron, thus releasing themselves from their fears and regrets and allowing them to move on with their lives. It's a bit like a New Year's resolution in reverse.

Once everyone has burned their lists, we make sure the cauldron is empty before filling it with wine, fresh autumn fruit, and spices. It is then hooked over the fire and allowed to heat through while we continue with our ritual: Remembering all those who have died in the name of the Craft, whether they practiced or not. Giving thanks to the animals who have sustained us in the last year, and wishing them a life further up the food chain next time around. Sharing our New Year's celebrations with our loved ones once again, and thanking the gods for our abundant harvest.

Once the brew in the cauldron is warm, we ladle some of it into our chalice and bless it along with the cakes, before sharing them while we discuss all things magical. Then we finish our ritual. As you can see, it wouldn't be quite the same without the cauldron.

Storm Black
The Alder Grove Coven,
www.thealdergrove.com

Making Magick—
Spellcraft & the Cauldron

Cauldrons, magick, and spells—oh my! It's so easy to conjure up that classic image of a Witch bent over a bubbling cauldron, adding ingredients and speaking incantations. But how realistic is that icon? It's time to find out for yourself! Let's explore what magick really is, look over some real working spells, and answer a few other questions you may have along the way.

What Is Magick?

Magick is the focusing of your intention and energy to influence or change something (you, your environment, other people, things, etc.). It is the art of changing consciousness in accordance with one's will. Consider that there is energy all around us—everything around us, living or inanimate, is made up of energy—all the way down to the molecular level of the atom. There's physical force and energy you can exert to change your environment, but that's just one kind. Your feelings and thoughts also can have a great deal of influence. Think about when you're having a bad day and things seem to keep getting worse, or when you're happy and your presence lightens the feel of the whole room around you. It's a kind of mind over matter. How we feel about our world and those around us does have a direct influence on so many things: the physical health of our bodies, our interactions with others, our homes, and where we work. Through the application of magick, we can harness that metaphysical energy to gain understanding and some level of control over these areas.

Why Are You Spelling Magick with a *k*?

When I first started out formally on my path, it was popular to use the *k* in *magick* to differentiate between the kind of metaphysical activities we do versus stage magic, sleight of hand, etc. The decision to add the *k* is a matter of choice, but personally I'm rather ambivalent about it—old habits die hard. (My spellchecker feels otherwise on the subject.)

Who Can Work Magick?

Anyone with a healthy imagination who can focus their intention can do magick. It is not aligned solely with any age, gender, or spiritual path—whether you're Pagan, Christian, Jewish, Hindu, or an atheist, you can work magick. Some people come by it more naturally than others, but it is indeed a skill that can be learned and developed over time with practice.

Is There Black/White, Good/Bad Magick?

Is there positive and negative wind, such as a summer breeze versus a hurricane? We tend to define things by how much trouble or damage they cause, but wind is just different kinds of movement. That summer breeze could come over a marsh first and bring waves of gnats with it. A hurricane could bring down old, rotted trees, creating room for new growth and development. I don't believe magick itself has any sort of a "color." Every spell will have a variety of results—intended and non-intended, positive and negative—depending on one's perspective. You simply cannot define magick solely by the intent, nor by the results.

Magick and Morality

I do believe you need to use common sense when working magick, and to truly consider what you're going to do before you do it. Make an effort to consider possible outcomes and consequences to avoid as many issues as possible. My partner Nathaniel introduced me to his "three rules for living," and

I believe they apply to all aspects of life—and that certainly includes working magick:

1) ***Take Care of Yourself.*** If you don't take care of your needs and respect yourself, it's going to be difficult to find anyone else who will.
2) ***Take Care of Others.*** When you can, help out others in need. Whether they need healing, protection, love, inspiration, or prosperity, a little goes a long way.
3) ***Don't Be a Jerk.*** It is technically possible to take care of yourself and others while still being a jerk about it. Listen to people, learn to receive, and respect the wishes of others. Don't go out of your way to hurt others.

Personal Power

The last thing I want to outline here before we get into spellcraft is the concept of personal power. You can definitely equate magick with prayer and even meditation, as they all require focus. Without getting into an argument about semantics, the big difference between the spells I'm presenting here and standard prayer is this: prayer is generally about asking a deity to do something for you, to petition their divine help because you can't make it possible. Spellcraft, for me, is about acknowledging the divine within yourself and believing in your own power to manifest change. It can certainly involve deities and spirits, but their part in it is more about assisting versus being the one to make the touchdown. (Yes, folks, I just used a sports analogy. Roll with me here.) Essentially, you are taking personal responsibility and acknowledging that *you* can bring about the change versus asking someone else to do it for you. The phrase "Goddess helps those who help themselves" comes to mind.

Sympathetic Magick and All That Stuff

The most common form of traditional spellcraft is sympathetic magick, which functions according to the concept that the microcosm can affect the macrocosm, or the part can affect or influence the whole. This kind of spellwork involves using items that imitate a person, place, action, or thing and/or correspond with something via a relationship, a physical connection, or some other similarity that can induce change. Spells that involve herbs, oils, candles, colors, sigils, poppets, jars, pouches, amulets, incense, talismans, and other items all generally work on the basis of the part/whole or correspondence relationship. I believe these items all work to help trigger various parts of your brain to enhance your focus, but they're not entirely necessary or mandatory for all workings. More stuff doesn't automatically produce better spells—sometimes (and actually I find more of the time) it's the simplest spell that works. So don't get too bogged down in details or fret if you don't have a specific item if you can find something else that works. Use what you have and be creative!

A Selection of Cauldron Spells

So what kind of magick can you make in your cauldron? Lots! You can use it to mix ingredients for satchels, teas, incenses, washes, and dustings. You can use it to release intentions or banish negativity by fire. I've crafted some spells to showcase some different ways you can use your cauldron, but this is by no means *all* of them—and if you're a careful reader, you will find plenty more throughout the book. I encourage you to let inspiration flow and devise your own spells too!

Tip: For the items listed in the spells (such as water, herbs, salt, etc.), you should adjust the amounts to accommodate the size of your cauldron and what makes you feel comfortable. Increasing the amount of an ingredient does not mean more power, especially if it overflows your cauldron! Most of the recommended amounts you'll find here were designed to work with a small to medium vessel.

Cleansing Spell to Purify an Object or Situation

Materials: A white candle; a tablespoon or small handful of vervain, rowan, and/or rue; an object to be cleansed (or a symbol for it); and enough water to completely cover the object. Perform from the full moon to the new moon.

Working: Place the object in the cauldron and light the candle. Waving the candle within the cauldron, say, *Fire blesses, fire purifies. The light brings new hope.*

Pour the water into the cauldron, saying, *Water blesses, water purifies. Through it we begin anew.*

Swirl in the herbs counterclockwise, saying, *Earth blesses, earth purifies. The past is swept away.*

Pull the object from the brew and blow onto it, then say, *Air blesses, air purifies. Through my breath this is born anew.*

Pour the brew down the drain or toilet, visualizing what has been washed away in the spell. Place the object on your altar or in a protected place for safekeeping.

Spell to Bring Prosperity or Build Something

Materials: A sunflower or squash seed (unprocessed); half a cup of water; incense, a bundle of dried herbs for burning, or a smudge stick; a cup of fresh earth; and a pot to grow in (or a container to transfer directly into the earth). Perform from the new moon to the full moon.

Working: Using your cauldron as a workbench, pour the earth into your cauldron and swirl it three times clockwise, thinking about the earth as a support structure and nourishment. Transfer the dirt to the pot or container. Bless the seed lightly with the smoke from the incense over the cauldron and put it in the potted earth. Pour the water into the cauldron, swirling it clockwise three times and thinking about how it will awaken the seed, then empty it carefully into the pot. Pressing the earth carefully around the seed, say, *This seed is the start of new prosperity. As it takes root and grows, so shall I prosper and my efforts bring fruit.*

Put the pot in a place where the sun can reach it and where you will remember to water it. Each time you visit it, visualize the working and the connection between the growing plant and prosperity.

Spell to Attract Money and Good Finances

Materials: Five shiny quarters, a tealight candle, water (enough to fill a third of the cauldron), and a teaspoon of basil, allspice, and cinnamon. Perform from the new moon to the full moon.

Working: Arrange the quarters in a star pattern in the bottom of your cauldron. Pour in the water and add the herbs, gently stirring clockwise. Light the candle and carefully place it in the water so that it floats on the surface. Repeat this chant five times: *Silver, spice, basil, and light, bring money now into my sight.*

Let the candle burn down completely, then pour or sprinkle the mixture by your front and back doors. Carry the quarters with you or place on your altar.

Awen Spell to Bring Creativity and Inspiration

Materials: A tablespoon each of lavender, anise seeds, and olive oil. Perform from the new moon to the full moon.

Working: This spell is for creating an anointing oil that you can place on yourself, around your work area, on tools, etc. Just a little will go a long way.

In your cauldron, drizzle in some olive oil and sprinkle in the lavender and anise seeds. With your dominant hand, mix the ingredients together in a clockwise motion, making a circle or star shape, five times in a row, while reciting, *May my heart, mind, body, and spirit be open to receiving and acting on inspiration. May I in turn create work that inspires others, making the circle whole. Wherever I anoint this oil, it shall be a beacon for inspiration. So shall it be!*

Allow the oil to sit for three nights, and collect it on the fourth morning into a container where you can use it daily. *Tip:* A funnel is your friend.

Self-Love Spell (Which in Turn Will Help Bring More Love into Your Life)

Materials: Enough rose petals and rosemary to fill a small pouch, a red button or bead on a string, and a small pouch (preferably red) to hold it all. Perform at the new or full moon ideally.

Working: So many people want a love spell to make someone else fall in love with them; meanwhile, they lack love for themselves. In order to attract love, you must have love. Combine in your cauldron the rose petals and rosemary. Holding the button or bead by the string above the cauldron, and moving in a slow counterclockwise motion, say, *I let go of self-hate. I let go of fear. I let go of pain.*

Then lower the bead/button into the herbs to make a trail. Moving clockwise, say, *I will be kind to myself. I will honor myself. I will believe in myself.*

Set the bead/button down into the herbs. Take the pouch and scoop up the bead/button and a good amount of the herbs into it. Carry it with you every day, preferably on your person. Sprinkle the remainder of the herbs by your doorway, so you'll walk through them.

Friendship Spell to Strengthen and Mutually Enhance a Bond

Materials: A teaspoon of cinnamon, a teaspoon of honey, half a cup of earth, a penny for each friend, and a seedling to plant and somewhere to plant it where it will be cared for (a small tree or hardy bush such as rosemary is a good idea).

Working: Sometimes friends decide they want to strengthen their relationship, especially if someone is moving away. In your cauldron, place the earth, followed by a teaspoon of honey and the pennies. Sprinkle the cinnamon on top and say, *Our friendship is our bond; it's the honey that holds us together. May we continue to be mindful of each other, respect each other, and keep each other in our memories. May our friendship continue to grow and bring us new blessings.*

Take the mixture and your seedling to the location where you will plant it and make room in the earth for the cauldron mix. Carefully scoop out the blend and place it into the earth, followed by the seedling. Water it and keep an eye on it. As it grows, your bond will grow as well.

Banishing Spell

Materials: A sheet of paper, a pen, a sprinkling of rue, and a lighter or matches. Best done from the full moon to the new moon.

Working: You can use this spell to get rid of any negative thing you need out of your life. Write down on the paper what you want to get rid of. Sprinkle the rue on top of it, then fold the paper in on itself in thirds. Then fold it again inward in thirds. (This would be a block of nine if you were to unfold it.) Place the folded paper in your cauldron and ready your match or lighter, then set the paper on fire, saying, *Be out, be gone, be away from my sight. Blessed rue, make it right.*

After the paper has burned (ideally to ashes), flush it down the toilet or throw the ashes into the sewer.

Making Magick—Spellcraft & the Cauldron

Protection Spell for the Home

Materials: A sprig/wand of rosemary, a cup of water, a teaspoon of sea salt, a sprinkle of sesame seeds, plus a tablespoon of rue, vervain, or mugwort.

Working: Use this spell to set up a protective energy barrier around your home. Pour the water into your cauldron, then add the sea salt, sesame seeds, and herbs. With your sprig/wand of rosemary, swirl the mixture clockwise, saying, *Hearth and home, window and door, protect this building from ceiling to floor.*

Start at the front door and move clockwise around the house, using the sprig/wand imbued with the mixture to anoint each door and window in a pentacle motion. If you wish, you can repeat the chant at every threshold.

A Binding Spell to Put Someone on Ice

Materials: A piece of paper, a pencil, a white string about a yard long, water (enough to fill a third of the cauldron), a generous teaspoon of vervain, a plastic bag that seals, and a freezer. Best done during the waning moon.

Working: Sometimes you just need to put somebody "on ice." That somebody can be a person bothering you or someone you love whom you want to help remotely who is harming themselves, deliberately or otherwise. With a pencil, write on the piece of paper the name of the person to be bound. Pour the water and vervain into the cauldron. Fold the paper up into thirds, and then into thirds again. (This would be a block of nine if you were to unfold it.) Then wrap the string around the paper, visualizing that whatever they are doing to cause harm will be stopped. Immerse it all in the cauldron water, soaking it thoroughly and continuing with the visualization for 1–3 minutes. Then pull it out and place the soaked cord-wrapped paper in the plastic bag and seal it. Then bring the baggie to its new home in the back of the freezer. Keep it there until the problem has been resolved. Once it is resolved, take the package from the freezer, remove the wrapped paper from the bag, and release it to the elements by burying or burning it. (Do *not* burn or bury the plastic bag! Recycle it!)

Burn and Release Cauldron Spell (Paper-Mache Cauldron Spell 1)

Materials: Strips of clean newsprint or similar lightweight scrap paper, writing implements, one part flour and one part water (the amount depends on the size of your intended vessel; just keep the parts equal, whether it's a half cup, one cup, etc.), a bowl and spoon for mixing, a cheap, wide paintbrush, a balloon, a container to hold the balloon secure, and a safe location in which to burn the cauldron. You can also add dried herbs, such as vervain (strength), patchouli (cleansing), and lavender (soothing), if you'd like. The best time for this spell is from the full moon through to the new moon.

Working: On the strips of paper, write down things you wish to banish/cleanse/release from your life. Next, mix together the flour and water, creating a paste. Add the herbs to the mixture (optional). Blow up the balloon to the size you'd like your cauldron to be, as it will be the base on which you build the cauldron. Wide-part up, set the balloon in a container that will keep it secure and upright while you work on it. Dip the written-on strips into the paste, and smooth them against the balloon using the paintbrush. As you add strips, cover the balloon with a bowl shape in mind, to create your cauldron. Let it dry completely, then pop the balloon gently to release the cauldron. To prepare your space appropriately, get your fire ready and center yourself. Call to mind the things you wrote on those slips of paper that you wish to remove safely from your life. Set the cauldron upon the fire, chanting, *Fire burn, fire cleanse, fire release! That which was written shall now cease!*

Honoring Memory Waterfire Cauldron Spell (Paper-Mache Cauldron Spell 2)

This spell is inspired by the traditions (including several Asian cultures, especially the Japanese) that honor ancestral spirits/deceased loved ones by setting lanterns on water with fire inside of them, as well as the idea of the Viking funeral (body/boat on fire). The spell is ideally released in an active body of water (such as an ocean or lake where it won't set anything else on fire or cause ecological damage) and then set on fire. If this is unavailable to you, then you can get creative with a basin of water or just use the fire aspect in your hearth/fireplace.

Materials: Copies of images/pictures of the ancestors/departed loved ones printed out on lightweight paper (don't burn originals!); fabric, ribbons, dried herbs, and similar materials that are easily burned and that remind you of the deceased (optional); one part flour and one part water (the amount depends on the size of your intended vessel; just keep the parts equal, whether it's a half cup, one cup, etc.); a bowl and spoon for mixing; a cheap, wide paintbrush; a balloon; a container to hold the balloon secure; a lighter; incense sticks or cones (optional); and a tealight candle or a small bundle of light kindling.

Working: Follow the instructions for Paper-Mache Cauldron Spell 1, using the photos, fabrics, etc., to build a cauldron of memories. Once dry, set off for your launch point so that you arrive near dusk. You have the choice of setting the vessel itself on fire (starting at the rim/lip edge) or setting a loose candle inside of the vessel—so that it will be a lantern that may eventually catch fire *before* it sinks. Or, most effectively, start a small kindling fire (add incense sticks or cones for both burning and aroma) inside the paper-mache cauldron and set the vessel off into the water, saying, *Hail to the spirits of those who have come before! You who have lit the way before us, may this pyre do you honor. May the current carry your memory, and may it flow strongly for future generations. That which is remembered lives. So mote it be!*

Stirring the Cauldron:
A Spell for Inspiration

WHAT THE WELSH tale of Ceridwen illustrates is the transformative power of her cauldron and how it can serve as a source of divine inspiration. When I'm having trouble putting together a ritual or rite for my Book of Shadows, I will sometimes gaze into a smaller version of Ceridwen's cauldron in an effort to find a solution. It's a rather simple ritual, but it's an effective one.

For this rite you will need a bowl, saucer, or large chalice full of water or wine, your Book of Shadows or a scratch pad, a pen, and an athame (though your finger will work if you don't have an athame). I prefer to do this working with a bit of witchy background music, though regular quiet works well too. Just make sure you are in a situation where you won't be disturbed by other people, your phone, etc. Many of the small rituals in this chapter don't call for a magick circle, but this one does. So before starting the rite, call upon the elements of earth, air, fire, and water, and cast a circle in whatever manner you are accustomed to.

Begin by inviting Ceridwen into your circle. You can simply meditate on her and her myth, say her name several times, or perform a traditional invocation such as this:

Great Ceridwen, goddess of the cauldron, mistress of the arts, loving mother, and giver of mystical inspiration, I ask you to join me this night in my circle. Help me to find my way and see the truth and power in my rites. Open the doors that lead to the mysteries of the Witch. Hail and welcome!

With Ceridwen now a part of your circle, pick up your athame and think about what it is you wish to have revealed. Are you stuck on a spell? A sabbat ritual? Whatever it is, think about that roadblock for a moment. Imagine yourself finding the solution to this problem.

As you hold your athame, feel the energy of your question build inside your body. Allow that energy to travel through you into your athame. While it's not imperative to use an athame here, as a tool of one's will it's a very effective way to deal with questions, and with its sharp and pointy tip it projects energy better than any other tool.

When the energy of your query reaches the tip of your athame, place it in the bowl and stir the water slowly in a clockwise motion eleven times. As you stir the water or wine, think about what it is you need revealed to you. Turn it over several times in your mind and imagine things associated with your question in the liquid being swirled by your athame. (For a bit of added energy you can place the cauldron on your altar's pentacle.)

After you've stirred your cauldron eleven times, begin saying the following lines. As you say each line, make one slow "stir" of the cauldron.

One for goddess Ceridwen eternal,
Two for her cauldron inspiration's source,
Three for the might of the night nocturnal,
Four for the power of Earth, nature's force,
Five times round for the answer that I seek,
Six for the potency of my true will,
Seven for the path of the Witch's mystique,
Eight times so that I might my quest fulfill,
Nine times now for the strength of night and day,
Ten times the water round my answers found,
Through Ceridwen's cup I have made my way.
Answers come to me now true and unbound.
Let me see the work that must be begun.
By our magical will it shall be done!
So mote it be!

Before looking into your Cauldron of Ceridwen, stir the waters within it eleven more times, feeling the magick of your rite and the power of the goddess surrounding you. As you look inside the waters of the cauldron, clear your mind and absorb whatever images might be there. If you don't see anything the first time, don't get discouraged; simply repeat the process again until you get the results you desire.

Whatever you see inside Ceridwen's waters, be sure to record them as quickly as you can (which is why I suggest bringing a Book of Shadows or notepad with you). If they don't make sense, write them down anyway and then review them again the next day. It's surprising what a good night's sleep can reveal.

Jason Mankey
Author, *The Witch's Athame*,
The Witch's Book of Shadows •
www.patheos.com/blogs/panmankey

Making Magick—Spellcraft & the Cauldron

Stirring the Cauldron:
Soaking a Spell

A GREAT USE for a cauldron is soaking a spell. My witchy group recently assembled a storage shed for our ritual gear and I wanted to consecrate it—and also lay down some heavy protection. During the time that I was helping to make the shed, I soaked two large High John the Conqueror roots in a small iron cauldron with a mixture of herbs, oils, powders, and general juju. Nightly stirrings by candlelight, murmured incantations, and intensely focused visualization occurred.

The cauldron itself was integral to the spell, as I imagined its solid permanence to be the stand-in for the metal structure: the cauldron contained the magick, just as our shed would contain our supplies. "Those without will stay without, and what's within will stay within."

A month later, when the shed was complete and stocked, we dug a hole on either side of the entrance, put the roots into the holes, poured the goopy mixture across the threshold between the two roots, and filled in the holes: anchored barrier—the "unwelcome" mat.

The intense zap that resulted from the cauldron soaking is still going strong eight years later. Recently a new member of the group closed the old padlock on the shed door, and we discovered that none of us could remember the combination to open it. We honestly had never bothered to lock the door in all of those years. To do so would have been redundant.

Angus McMahan
**Angus McMahan is a gregarious
solitary who can usually be found
playing strange drums strangely.
He also writes down words on occasion. •
www.angus-land.com**

Cauldron Magick FAQ

Let's look at some common questions about cauldrons.

Does Your Cauldron Have a Memory?

Myth: The cauldron can hold a memory of every kind of magick ever performed in it, so be careful what kind of magick you do.

First off, every kind of magick has positive and negative consequences, regardless of your initial intent. Unless the cauldron was crafted from scratch with a specific intention in mind, it can always be cleansed—physically and metaphysically. You should be more concerned with physically mixing activities that don't agree with each other—such as cooking meals and mixing flying ointments in the same cauldron without proper washing (and even then I would recommend using different cauldrons). If you believe your cauldron holds a memory of every thing that was ever done in it, then I would be far more concerned about the time you overcooked the pasta than the intention of your working.

Do You Need to Cast a Magick Circle First Before Doing a Spell?

It depends on the practitioner, what the work is, and where the spellcraft is being done:

- If you blessed your home and/or have a specific area that you always work in, then you've already established that space as sacred.
- If you have to do a spell somewhere you don't normally work, then it's a good idea to cast a circle to define that space for the time of the working. Some practitioners can simply do this in their mind, and it stems from pulling in the sense of their own space wherever they are.

- If you're doing the kind of magick where you're summoning spirits, entities, and so forth in a ceremonial sense, then, yes, casting a circle first is generally a good idea, but pretty much everything in this book is focused on practical magick. If you're doing extensive divining work that involves ancestors, spirits, and other beings, then it may be wise to take that extra step.

The Seer's Cauldron

Divination is another very handy use for the cauldron. In this chapter, we'll join the legions of our ancestors who all sought to reveal the future. We'll define some of the many practices utilized over the centuries and also find some modern-day methods of our own to employ.

The Ancient Art of Divination

Human beings have been obsessed with seeing into the future since we first became aware of linear time and consequence. There are hundreds of different methods that have been employed all over the world to catch a glimpse of what the Fates might have in store for us. From observing the movements of animals and the weather to using carefully devised systems like the Tarot and runes, there are so many options, as well as ways to interpret them. Divining the future has long been linked with those who work with the supernatural (shamans, priests, oracles, healers, Witches, magicians, etc.), as it's seen as tapping into another realm. But as we can tell from the popularity of the Ouija board, Tarot, crystal readings, etc., most people are indeed curious about divination and wish to try it out! So no matter how you define yourself, I've included some cauldron-based methods for you to try.

It's rather easy to see how cauldrons came naturally for use in divination. Imagine stirring a brew for hours on end (a magical potion, or maybe just dinner), staring into the bubbling swirls and making repetitive motions with your body; you're quite likely to go into a trance. Divination works best when you can clear the mind, soften your focus on the world around you, and allow yourself to look inward (the true sense of the term *inner eye*).

Luckily, I have several suggestions for you that don't involve spacing out while you brew a spell or make dinner (which not only is dangerous on several levels but could potentially ruin whatever you're working on). Some of these methods require very little setup, while others do require you to exercise common sense and follow safety protocol—as to be expected when working with fire in *any* form.

The seer's cauldron

Many of these techniques are hundreds (if not thousands) of years old, yet there is little information regarding interpretations for them. I recommend keeping a journal of your workings, noting the time, day, lunar phase, and conditions—as well as any particular topic or question you may be seeking an answer to—and record the results. We each have our own personal mythos, symbols, and cultural baggage, so trust your instincts.

Note: Whether divining by flame, incense, or wax, always be sure to work in a properly ventilated room, place your cauldron on a fireproof surface, and have extinguishing tools nearby *before* you start divining!

A Brief Glossary of Related Divination Terms

Carromancy: Divination by observing the melting of wax (typically a tapered candle or votive as it melts, or how long it burns for)

Ceromancy: Divination by the dripping of wax onto a surface of water and observing the shapes it makes

Cleromancy: Divination by casting lots

Eleomancy: Divination by dripping oil onto water and observing the shapes it makes upon the surface

Hydromancy: Divination involving water, including observing still water, movement, and evaporation

Libanomancy: Divination by interpreting the shapes and movement of smoke/incense

Pyromancy: Divination by fire, which can involve gazing into the flames all the way through to examining the end result of a fire (ashes, smoke marks, etc.)

Scrying: Divination by looking into a dark surface, pool, or mirror

Before You Start Performing Divination: To Use Ritual or Not?

It is a good idea to prepare yourself body, mind, and spirit before performing divination. How you choose to go about this depends a great deal on your personal and spiritual beliefs. Ritual can be very elaborate or very simple—at the root, it is all about setting an order to things to create comfort and awareness. I suggest having a light yet satisfying meal and being well hydrated before you start—there is nothing more annoying than trying to achieve a trancelike state with your stomach grumbling or when feeling thirsty. I advise against using alcohol beforehand, as it tends to be a psychic suppressant. (However, if a small nip of something truly helps you relax, and you're of legal drinking age, then do what works for you.)

Many a path recommends protecting yourself before divining. By protection, I mean metaphysically setting up sacred space for you to work in, calling in protective spirits/saints/deities, or wearing some sort of spiritual protection. This can be done by setting up a magick circle (see chapter 5), lighting a white candle, anointing yourself with an oil/essence associated with protective duties, or wearing an amulet or talisman designed to shield and protect (a pentacle, cross, saint medallion, etc.). Most importantly, respect yourself and respect any possible entities you may be working with.

Lastly, after you finish your work, take time to breathe, ground, make note of your findings, and clean up after yourself. It's irresponsible to go through the process of divination but then leave a mess to clean up later. Complete your working properly by cleaning your cauldron, extinguishing any candles, and putting things anyway. You'll feel better for it.

Tip: Sometimes it's handy to practice divination with a like-minded friend. They can assist you in preparing and going into a trancelike state, then ask you questions and record what you say.

Scrying the Dark Mirror

About: Using your cauldron filled with water as a dark scrying mirror is one of the simplest and often most effective forms of divination. It takes very little to get started, and it can be done anywhere, at any time, given you have the space and peace to do it. Some people find entering trance quite easy, while others must practice to get it down. Be patient, and be sure to give yourself the advantages necessary to be successful by preparing properly.

Materials: A black or dark-colored cauldron, enough water to fill the cauldron (measured and ready in a pitcher or glass), and something to focus on—traditionally this would be the reflection of the full moon in your cauldron, but a silver coin or similarly colored stone (moonstone, quartz, etc.) placed in the bottom of the cauldron will do the trick as well. (The reflection of the full moon wins extra cool points.)

Preparation: As you won't be burning anything, you don't have to worry about placing the cauldron on a fireproof surface. It's best to work in a quiet room or area where you won't be disturbed or distracted by others or electronics (silence your phone!). It's best to sit, so either get some pillows and get comfy on the floor so you can look down into the cauldron, or find a table/chair setup that will accomplish the same comfortably. Some people prefer to scry at the new or full moon, but I believe that when you've got a question it's best to get to work ASAP.

Practice: Take a deep breath and hold it for a count of three seconds, then release it. Repeat this in-hold-out pattern two more times, holding the second breath for six seconds and the third one for nine seconds before releasing each. Bring to mind the question or situation you wish to divine, and place the coin/crystal in the cauldron or position it to catch the available moonlight if that's an option for you. Pour the water slowly into the cauldron and focus on the coin or reflecting light. Allow your eyes to slowly lose focus and soften, and be patient. Take note of what images and thoughts come to mind.

FAQ: Where Should the Water Come From? That's completely up to you. You can use water from the tap, boil water to purify it (then let it cool), purchase commercially distilled water, and/or ritually prepare it. I know Witches who collect (a lot of) snow on certain occasions (full moon, new moon, the solstice), bottle it, bless it, and save it for use in ritual. If you live somewhere devoid of snow and are feeling adventurous (or connected to a specific body of water you live near), you could collect water from a spring, river, lake, bay, or ocean—just be aware of the microbes you are harvesting along with it. If you plan on keeping it around, then consider boiling it and then storing it in the fridge—properly labeled! Otherwise, using water that's readily available to you (from the kitchen sink) is no crime. If you have the time and the desire to do so, here's a simple water blessing you can do without leaving your home.

Simple Water Blessing

Near the full moon, fill a pot or tea kettle with water from the tap, and bring it a rolling boil for 1–3 minutes. Then allow it to cool, and transfer it to a jar and lid it. (I prefer to use large recycled Mason jars; the pasta sauce variety works well.) Hold the jar in your hands and concentrate on the future being made clear to you. Then place the jar on your altar (if you have one), on a windowsill that you can see the moon out of (without the jar being at risk of being knocked over by pets or children), or outside if the weather permits (not when it's freezing outside!). Allow the water to "soak up" the moon for three days. Then it's ready to use!

The Transporter Effect (Glittermancy)

About: This divination method may seem a tad unconventional, but it's both fun and effective. I call it the "transporter effect" in homage to *Star Trek* (the original series) and how the special effects team used glitter to create the teleport effect. Older methods involved sand, silt, or dirt—the key thing you are looking for is contrast, so if you'd like to try one of those, be sure to use a container that will contrast enough against the material.

Materials: A black or dark-colored cauldron, enough water to fill the cauldron (measured and ready in a pitcher or glass), a vial of silver glitter (the finer and more sand-like, the better), and something to stir with that won't be too visually distracting—like a clear plastic spoon or black chopstick.

Preparation: See "Scrying the Dark Mirror" in the previous section, with the added caution that glitter has a habit of getting everywhere. You have been warned.

Practice: Take a deep breath and hold it for a count of three seconds, then release it. Repeat this in-hold-out pattern two more times, holding the second breath for six seconds and the third one for nine seconds before releasing each. Bring to mind the question or situation you wish to divine, and pour the water into the cauldron. Slowly begin to stir the water with one hand, and with the other hand slowly pour the glitter into the cauldron. Stop stirring and watch the patterns and shapes that the glitter creates. Swirl again as needed until satisfied. Take note of what images and thoughts come to mind.

Tip: Since glitter can be messy *and* brings up several ecological issues concerning its disposal, you can let the water evaporate naturally out of the cauldron and collect the glitter to use again when it's dry (preferably stored in a safe place where your pets won't drink it). If you're using a cauldron that you can heat up on the stove, you can evaporate the water more quickly, but keep an eye on it so you don't melt the glitter to the cauldron.

Grandmom's Way—Practical Kitchen Witchery Meets Divination

You can perform eleomancy (divination by dripping oil onto water) when you're preparing to boil pasta. Whether you're boiling the water in a cauldron or one of its more modern cousins, you can easily take a moment to ground and center yourself, pour salt and olive oil into your pot of water, stir it counterclockwise three times, and observe the shapes it makes before heating the water. The bonus of this practice is that not only can you practice divination, but the resulting water gets used immediately to make a meal! (Then you can practice *pastamancy* based on the outcome of your work. Hint: if your pasta clumps together, that's generally not a good omen.)

The Dice Cup

About: This form of divination involves what is known as *cleromancy*, which refers to methods that involve casting lots: runes, stones, bones, shells, sticks, etc. There are two methods: *dry*, which involves using a large square of cloth (big enough to cover the inside of the cauldron) made of something soft yet sturdy, such as velvet or flannel, and *wet*, which involves filling the cauldron with water. Which method you use will depend on how fragile or impervious to water your casting system is. Semiprecious stones and other rocks, bones, and shells may meet an untimely demise if they come into contact with the sides of the cauldron too harshly. Wood, handpainted items, and anything water-soluble will also not meet a good end when submerged. If you're unsure, then experimenting with resin, metal, nut shells, etc., could be a great way to go. If you have a marker and a pile of pistachio nuts, you could improvise a pretty awesome set of casting pieces!

Materials: Any kind of cauldron, sized to accommodate whatever materials you may be casting. If you go for the dry method, acquire a square of cloth big enough to cover your cauldron and leave "ears" sticking out of the vessel. You want this cloth to be a cushion between the items to be cast and the walls of the cauldron, but nothing too stiff, so choose carefully. Velvet, velour, heavy cotton, and flannel are all good options. If you go for the wet method, you'll need enough water to fill the cauldron—and, of course, whatever system you'll be using to cast.

Preparation: See "Scrying the Dark Mirror" earlier in this chapter. If you're using a cloth, make sure it's clean, and have a good source of light nearby.

Dry Practice: Settle yourself in, and place the cloth in the cauldron so that it covers the inside yet has enough extra fabric poking out for you to grab or fold over. Take a deep breath and hold it for a count of three seconds, then release it. Repeat this in-hold-out pattern two more times, holding the second breath for six seconds and the third one for nine seconds before releasing each. Bring to mind the question or situation you wish to divine, and pour your stones into the cauldron. Close one hand over the fabric so that it's "lidded," and with the other hand grasp the cauldron and gently swirl the whole thing in three slow counterclockwise circles while concentrating on your question. Stop, let the stones come to a rest inside, put the cauldron down, and open up the fabric. Examine the formation inside to divine your answer.

Wet Practice: Take a deep breath and hold it for a count of three seconds, then release it. Repeat this in-hold-out pattern two more times, holding the second breath for six seconds and the third one for nine seconds before releasing each. Bring to mind the question or situation you wish to divine, and pour the water into the cauldron. With your stones in your dominant hand (both hands are fine if you need more space OR you could put them in a pouch or small container that you can hold), swirl the stones gently three times counterclockwise and drop them into the cauldron. Allow them to settle and then examine the results. This application of blending hydromancy and cleromancy can be quite fascinating and fun!

Tip: After you're done divining with water that is clean (no glitter, no oil, no wax, etc.), instead of pouring the water down the drain, use it to water plants in your home or outside.

The Flaming Cauldron

The following practices all involve fire, either through candles, smoke, or incense. Unlike in the previous exercises that didn't require the use of fire, be sure to take necessary precautions to properly handle fire and smoke. Perform your divination in a well-ventilated area, placing your cauldron on or over a fire-proof surface. Have the lid or a proper size cover handy, and avoid wearing easily flammable clothing.

Wax and Water Method

About: This method involves ceromancy—that is, divination by dripping wax onto a surface of water and observing the shapes it makes.

Materials: A cauldron, a votive candle in an easy-to-handle container (tealights can be used but should be placed in a secondary holder, as the thin metal they're contained in will get hot and hard to handle), enough room-temperature water to fill the cauldron (measured and ready in a pitcher or glass), and something to light the candle with.

The cauldron aflame

Preparation: Make sure the area you'll be working in is fireproof and also properly covered to prevent any accidental wax spillage. A good option is to cover a table that you can comfortably stand at with aluminum foil. You can also choose to

189

sit as long as you can see over the cauldron and move about enough to pour the wax. Since you'll be working with an open flame and melted wax, it's a good idea to make sure pets and children won't disturb you. As with the earlier described techniques, choose the space and time wisely to conduct your divination.

Practice: Take a deep breath and hold it for a count of three seconds, then release it. Repeat this in-hold-out pattern two more times, holding the second breath for six seconds and the third one for nine seconds before releasing each. Light the candle while thinking about the question or situation you wish to divine, and place it in the cauldron. Meditate on the flame, and focus on your breath. When ready (ideally after having given the candle enough time to melt), remove the candle (still lit) from the cauldron and put it aside, within easy reach. Pour in the water and let it settle. When you feel ready, gently but quickly pour the melted wax onto the surface of the cauldron and blow out the candle. Observe the shapes the wax has made upon the surface, and divine your answer.

Note: The neat thing about this method is that you can fish the wax out from the water and put it aside to document it, and/or save the wax to melt down again if you're into candle making. *Don't pour the wax down the sink or onto plants!*

Tip: You can light the candle ahead of time, to get more melted wax, but I recommend doing it as part of a ritual preparation or integrating it into a spell before you sit down to divine. You can also use this method to give you insight into how the spell may turn out, if it's centered on a candle working.

Candle Working and Divination

Another way to work with divination and candles in your cauldron is to incorporate them with spellcraft to determine the potential outcome or effectiveness of a spell. Candle working is a very simple kind of sympathetic magick that requires minimal fuss. As you prepare your candle and burn it, you focus on your goal. When it is finished, the energy is released into the world. By burning the candle in your cauldron while performing the work, you can divine how successful your spell will be.

Getting Started: If you're buying candles, inspect them before purchasing. Note the scent (if any) to see if it works for your purpose, look at how decent the wick is, and check the overall condition of the candle—no breaks, bends, cracks, etc. (Note: If you're extra crafty, you could also specially make your own candles!) You can use any sort of candle you wish, but I recommend short taper candles, tealights, or birthday candles (as long as they're not "dripless") for a quick burning of a one-time spell. (Some candle magick calls for the repeated burning of a candle over an extended period of time, so a devotional candle or similar votive would be more suitable for those workings.)

Candle Spell Considerations

Here are some things to think about when considering your candle spell.

What Is Your Goal?

Is your goal realistic? Can you visualize it happening? What are the possible outcomes and consequences?

What Is the Moon Doing?

The moon phase can affect the flow of your work. If you're doing a healing spell and the moon is waxing, you'll want to focus on increasing good health. Inversely, during the waning moon you can focus on the banishing of the illness. I'm a big fan of doing the work when you feel it's necessary, so if the moon phase doesn't seem ideal, look at your problem from a different perspective to get the energy working with you.

What Color of Candle?

The following color associations come from my own experience. If these don't relate to you, work with your own personal color correspondences.

Red: Passion, sex, love, issues of family, blood

Orange: Harvest, positive energy, promise

Yellow: Friendship, to overcome depression, cheerfulness

Green: Prosperity, health, growth

Blue: Personal power, healing, knowledge and understanding

Purple: The divine, the Fey, the unseen, blending

Pink: Love, security, gentleness, youth

Brown: Grounding, earth, renewal, clarity

Black: Binding, banishing, crone and warrior aspects, death mysteries, balance

White: All-purpose, cleansing, purity, focus, balance, peace

Other Options for Your Candle

- You can write on your candle or carefully carve your intention in it.
- You can inscribe it with symbols associated with your goal.
- You can anoint it with essential oils that resonate with your work.

A Solid Base

Lastly, be sure to acquire a secure base to place your candle upon. You could melt the bottom of the candle and fix it to the bottom of your cauldron before you start, but wax can get *really* messy. So unless the cauldron is always used for candle magick, you may want to line the base of it with a small mirror or metal foil, and make sure the candle can stand properly in its own holder, within the cauldron.

Manifesting!

Once you've gotten the candle ready and have prepared your work area to make sure it's safe for fire use, it's time to make some magick! As with the previous divination methods we've discussed, settle in and take some deep breaths. Focus on your goal, visualize it clearly in your mind, and light the candle, placing it in the cauldron. As it burns, keep your mind on the candle and watch it carefully, making notes.

Observe

- The size of the flame—does it burn strongly or weakly? This can indicate how well your working will turn out.
- Flame movement—does it sputter like it's fighting, or is it languid and slow? Or does it seem to dance about with excitement?
- The speed at which the candle is burning—is it fast, slow, or steady? Is it a ten-minute candle burning out in five minutes or lasting for half an hour? This could indicate how fast the spell will progress—or how long the goal itself will last.
- Wax shapes—does the melting wax make any interesting patterns or specific forms or flows?

As with all divination, your interpretation will be best guided by your intuition. Once the candle has burned out (this is why it's a good idea to get a quick-burning candle), take three deep breaths, doing one last visualization of your spell as you do so. Then clean up after yourself and carry on.

Fire, Smoke, and Incense Divination

Out of all of the divination methods, I'd say that pyromancy and libanomancy are the most hazardous. So if you chose to use them, *please* be careful *what* you burn and *where* you burn it, and be sure to do it in a *well-ventilated area* and have *fire-prevention methods* within easy reach.

Note: I know it may seem like I make a lot of warnings about safety, but I've seen a lot of things go wrong very quickly over the years. Sure it can be funny *after* the fact when you set your table on fire or burned something that caused an allergic reaction, but my hope is that you will make more fun mistakes instead that don't have potentially harmful side effects.

Pyromancy

This method involves building a fire, gazing into it, and possibly also examining the remains of it once it has burned out. If you're going to build a fire in your cauldron, then I highly recommend doing it outside in a fire-safe area—and in a cast-iron cauldron. If this is not a viable option for you, then perhaps explore this type of divination sans cauldron the next time you're at a campfire or bonfire. I also don't recommend divination with a fire involving Epsom salts and alcohol—you want something that has its basis in wood. Part of achieving the trance state involves watching how the kindling moves and changes shape as it burns.

Materials: To kindle your fire, you can choose specific woods aligned with divination or a specific deity. Woods most commonly associated with visions include rowan, willow, apple wood, hawthorn, and poplar. Another interesting option is to collect small pieces of dry driftwood from the ocean or other salty body of water. Wood that has been soaking in salt for a while can burn some unusual and mesmerizing colors! You may also wish to have some herbs on hand (such as sandalwood or mugwort), set in a small bowl, to toss on the fire.

Preparation: Set up your area properly for fire tending, safety, and prevention, and make sure you have something comfortable to sit on.

Practice: With all of your materials handy, take three deep breaths. Focus on the purpose of your divination and carefully build your fire (start small!). Once the fire has begun, settle into a comfortable position and fix your vision on the flames. You may be able to achieve a trance state by watching the fire for as long as it lasts. Or once the fire is going, you can ask your question and toss a small amount of the herbs onto the fire. Watch how the fire responds to the herbs. Do this for as long as you need to, then conclude your practice. If the fire isn't burned out yet, gently place the lid on top of the cauldron to smother it.

Libanomancy

This involves interpreting the shapes and movement of smoke or incense. As this divination method is most commonly done with a charcoal disc, it's much easier to control it as well as do it indoors—as long as it doesn't set off your smoke alarm. If you're unsure about how sensitive the alarm is, and you live in an apartment complex or in a household with a lot of other people whom you're going to inconvenience if it does go off, then don't be that person—do it outdoors instead, or opt for a non-smoke method. The aroma can definitely be a wonderful sensation, as the sense of smell can trigger powerful memories, but remember that the purpose of this divination method is to watch the smoke, not be immersed *in* it.

Materials: Sand or salt to fill the bottom of the cauldron, charcoal disc, incense blend, matches or lighter. You can make your own incense blend, or purchase one from an occult shop. Ingredients sometimes found in divining incenses: mugwort, sandalwood, laurel, vervain, peppermint, sweet basil, witch hazel, centaury, myrrh, frankincense, dragon's blood, benzoin, rue.

Preparation: Set up your area properly for fire safety and prevention, and make sure you have something comfortable to sit on. Fill the base of the cauldron with sand or salt to insulate it against the charcoal disc.

Practice: With all of your materials handy, take three deep breaths. Focus on the purpose of your divination, light the charcoal disc, and place it in the center of the cauldron. Consider what you're divining as the charcoal heats up, then place a small amount of the incense upon it. Watch the smoke. Does it move quickly or slowly? Is it one continuous stream or multiple threads? Does it make any other shapes? Add incense as needed. When you're done, smother the charcoal by covering it with the sand and/or lidding the cauldron.

Note: I have purposely not included any forms of divination that involve burning or steaming entheogens (potentially poisonous/toxic herbs) to achieve an altered state for divination through inhalation. These methods should be attempted only if you are in excellent physical condition and have a solid understanding of herbalism and a healthy respect for the spiritual properties of those herbs. They are powerful methods, but inappropriate or uneducated use can cause severe illness and even death. While several mid-twentieth-century writers have mentioned the obscure possibility of unknown herbs being tossed on a steaming or burning cauldron to "ride to the sabbat" (aka visionflight, spiritwalking, out-of-body experience), much research has been done in recent years to fully explore flying ointments (herbal blends rubbed onto the skin). So if this practice piques your interest, I have included some suggested resources at the end of this book for further study (see the "Regarding Herbs and Magick" section).

On Chants, Chanting, and Music

Some people love chants, while others prefer absolute quiet, and still others require soft music or some sort of white noise (static, humming, a fan, etc.) in the background. Chanting, rhymes, and similar forms of mantras can help the chatty brain relax and focus on pattern and breath. Those who are adept at doing this naturally may find quiet, music, or white noise far more effective. (Just remember to create a repeating playlist if you use music, or you may get some surprises!) What works best for you is for you to discover. I've included some chants here for you to consider, but if you're inspired, I thoroughly encourage you to try writing your own. You can begin repeating these after doing the three breaths, and stop when you feel comfortable.

- *Power of darkness, power of light, grant me the gift of inner sight.*
- *By the flame and by the fire, give me the answer I require.*
- *Being of smoke, creature of air, grant to me clear vision fair.*
- *Goddess moon, lunar bright, by your power bring me sight.*
- *All that ebbs and all that flows, lunar wisdom through me grow.*
- *Stone and metal, shell and bone, reveal to me what the Fates have sewn.*

chapter
8

Thinking Outside the Cauldron

So far we've covered some rather typical, traditional, and downright classic uses for cauldrons. But what about the other hidden cauldrons lurking in your home? No, really! I bet you have at least two unexpected cauldrons in your residence right this minute, maybe even right behind you! Let's meet them and discover how to bring some extra magick into your daily life.

Cauldron Cousins and the Unconventional Cauldron

It's fascinating to look at the path of civilization alongside the development of utilitarian design.

Since the earliest days of civilization, human beings have struggled between creating and possessing objects that are necessary for basic survival and making those that embellish and enhance our existence.

The earliest cave people used every part of a kill to further their existence, yet they also took the time to fashion deities from stone and bone and cover their walls with glorious imagery. Societies that migrated and traveled to maintain life mastered the art of combining function and artistry, finding multiple uses for the same item to cut down on weight yet making it beautifully crafted. Taking on a sedentary lifestyle meant there was more space to put things, allowing for the saving of resources as well as the room to find other ways to solve problems and perhaps save time. The people who adopted agriculture and animal husbandry as a way of life often founded cities that excelled in the making and use of artistic objects—allowing for items to be highly elaborate and ritualized. More room meant more space for specialized items versus needing to use an all-purpose object to maximize storage and living areas.

While the cauldron itself has undergone few changes over time—with those upgrades occurring mainly in the structural material and physical construction—advances in technology and the human compulsion to make *stuff* has spawned many cousins. Once we got past a way of living that required or mandated having a single multipurpose pot, many of the cauldron's cousins were born.

We can divide the cousins into four categories of specialization (with some crossover):

Preparing and Cooking Liquids: Hotpots, fondue pots, Crock-Pots, tea kettles, mortars and pestles, distillers, broilers, etc.

Fire and Food: Barbeques and grills, stoves and ovens, drying dishes, smokers, etc.

Light and Warmth: Braziers, furnaces, stoves, oil lamps, fire pots and pits, etc.

Cleaning and Washing Treatments: Washers, steamers, bathtubs, hot tubs, etc.

An entire book could be written about the history and development of just *one* of these items. My point in listing them is to get you thinking outside of the cauldron. If you think magick can happen only with a traditional cauldron, think again! I'm going to introduce you to some unconventional cauldrons that may be lurking in your home right *now*! (Creeper cauldrons!)

The Blessed Bathtub

I'm going to start with our favorite cauldron in our entire household: the bathtub. The best feature of the old house we currently live in is that it has a five-foot-long and very deep claw-foot cast-iron tub. Sure, there's a powerful shower head and decent-size plastic tub in the other bathroom, but this tub is pure magick. Both my partner and I can fit in it together and still have room for all three cats to stare at us disbelievingly from the side. (Look, I told you about the time we set a table on fire during a Samhain ritual, so I can brag about the tub. We're even now.)

Cauldrons have been used for cleaning for quite some time—remember Odysseus's bath in the giant cauldron at Circe's? But now we have indoor plumbing, hot water heaters (another kind of cauldron!), and the almighty indoor tub—which is essentially a giant cauldron that you can do some fabulous workings with.

There are several different ways you can do spellcraft and ritual in the tub using salts and herbal infusions. First of all, you should always start with a nice clean tub, and it doesn't hurt if the rest of the bathroom is clean as well. You are welcome to embellish the tub with incense and candles that work with your spell as well—some folks like to set up a temporary altar and cast a circle too, but that's totally up to you. Apart from the preparation of your infusions, the rest of the procedure involves setting your body and mind in the right frame.

A bathtub set for spellcrafting

Before starting the bath, take three slow breaths and focus on your purpose. For spells working with increasing certain energies in your life, you'll want to be sure to get into the tub as you start the bath, so you can physically feel the water rise and take in the aromas of the herbs. While you're in the bath, keep your concentration on the working—this is not your typical bath! This is not the time to read a book or play on your phone. When you're ready, take another three deep breaths, unplug the tub, and get out, imagining the patting-off process as "sealing" those energies into your skin.

Making Herbal Infusions and Salts

For your sanity, and for the sake of that fabulous indoor plumbing, the methods outlined here require minimal cleanup. It's wonderfully romantic to soak in a stew of rose petals and herbs while you're actually in it (and they make great photos on Instagram), but nothing takes the edge off magick like trying to get herbal debris off your body and out of your hair and having to wipe and scour your tub as soon as you're done. How to avoid that mess? Custom-make your own herbal infusion or bath salts! Here's how.

The Giant Tea Bag

The easiest method is to take or make a large muslin bag about 4 x 6 inches large or so, and load it with about an ounce of dried herbs—they will expand when wet, so don't overfill the bag. Tie it securely and place it in the tub as you start the water. The herbal essences will filter into the tub just like a tea bag in a cup. You can also add a few drops of an essential oil if you want even more aroma.

The Two-Part Infusion
Start with a good-size pot of freshly boiled water and add in your herbs—they can be dried or fresh, or a mix of both. The exact balance depends on your personal preference, but a half ounce of herbs to a pint of water is a good starting ratio. Put the lid on the pot and allow the herbs to steep for at least 15–20 minutes. Strain the herbs from the water, carefully saving the water and setting aside the herbs for composting. Add the herbally infused water to your bath, and there you go!

Tip: If you have a shower unit and no tub, you can modify the use of the two-part infusion by pouring it onto yourself or using a washcloth to squeeze it onto yourself in the shower stall. Just make sure it's not too hot first!

The Salt of the Tiny Sea
For this method you'll need some Epsom salts, table salt, essential oils, and an airtight container. Take equal parts Epsom and table salts and place them in your jar. Add 8–12 drops of essential oil, put the lid on, give it a good shake to distribute everything, and let the mix stew for an hour. Then it's ready to use. Start with small amounts (¼ cup or so of

each salt) to see how you like the mix, and alter as needed. Don't forget to journal your experiment so you know the amounts for next time.

Recipes for Herbal Infusions and Salts

I've included three suggestions of herbs for each kind of working. You can choose to use one or all of them, or add herbs from your own practice. These are just to get you started, but do keep in mind potential allergies. Not all herbs are nice when they come in contact with delicate parts.

Cleansing

To purify yourself, whether in preparation for a ritual or to rid yourself of a habit, feeling, issue, etc.

Suggestions: Valerian, rue, mugwort

Protection

For protection for any purpose—physical, psychic, mental, etc.

Suggestions: Vervain, St. John's wort, rue

Love

To draw love to you by starting with self-love.

Suggestions: Rose petals or rosehips, sweet basil, lavender

Prosperity and Good Luck

To bring in money and/or work opportunities and to draw luck to you.

Suggestions: Patchouli, anise seed, rosemary

Serenity and Healing
For recovery, de-stressing, and peace of mind.
   Suggestions: Lavender, mugwort, ginger

Divination/Psychic Awareness
To encourage psychic insight and better divining skills.
   Suggestions: Mugwort, marigold petals, mint

The Wondrous Washing Machine

While we're on a cleaning kick, let's discover some new ways of looking at the washing machine—doing laundry might now become fun! The cauldron was often used to wash clothes, treat fabrics and fibers, and prepare textiles—which included dyeing them. Keeping in mind that not everyone has a washer in their home, but may share one in a rental unit or use the laundromat, I'm going to focus my attention on a relatively safe kind of working that can be done in a single use of a machine: the herbal infusion.

So, you may be wondering, why would you want to infuse your clothes with an herbal concoction? Clothes are another layer of protection and, as many fashion designers know, are a type of physically transforming glamour. Imagine any of the herbal baths we just covered bringing those same energies to the clothes you are wearing. It really kicks the magick up another level, because it's another reminder of your intention.

You have several options to infuse your clothes. You can pour a jar of your prepared two-part infusion water in the machine with your clothes. You can prepare a very sturdy cloth bag, sewn tightly closed with herbs, and toss it in with your load of wash. Or you can use one of those washer balls (designed to slow-release detergent) and fill it with herbs. If the holes are big enough to let herbal particles out, then first place them in a muslin tea bag, then place the bag inside the washer ball. You don't want herbal debris getting all over the washing machine and clothes.

The herbs aren't going to clean your clothes, so this may be a special process you do only with some already clean clothes that you plan to wear to a job interview, on a date, or to an important meeting. If you want double-duty, then I suggest using one of those "free and clear" detergents that don't have additional chemicals, perfumes, etc. Also, be mindful not to combine light-colored clothes with herbs that will possibly stain. If you're unsure about an herb, do a two-part infusion and see what color the water is after you've drained it. If it's clear or mostly clear, you should be good to go.

Be sure to remove your herbal pouch or ball before putting the clothes in the dryer. I don't recommend trying this method with your dryer, as the herbs may burn or catch on fire.

Old-School Option: Use a large cauldron or basin to soak your clothes in the herbal infusion during the appropriate moon cycle (such as during the full moon for an evening). Then wring them out and air-dry them.

Tea Cup and Kettle

Now that we're squeaky clean, let's head on over to the kitchen and make ourselves a nice cup of warm goodness. I'm a tea drinker and my partner is primarily a coffee drinker, but we both gather round the electric kettle to craft our respective brews. And I must sing to you the praises of the electric kettle!

Over the years, I have used a variety of methods to heat up my water—from the traditional tea kettle on the stove at home to microwaving mugs of water at work (don't judge me!). Being an artist and designer, I would constantly get caught up in whatever art I was working on and forget about the tea kettle (that had a crap whistle so I wouldn't hear it go off) or that mug in the microwave. Then, a few years ago, I was visiting my friends Anaar and Onyx, and they had in their kitchen a truly magical device: an electric kettle on a simple base. You just fill it with water, turn it on, and just a short while later, hot water! Witchcraft! It's both energy-efficient and fast, so I don't forget about making my tea or have to keep reheating water over and over again.

Thinking Outside the Cauldron

Now that I've just probably caused an increase in the value of electric kettle stock, let's talk about making magick with any kind of kettle—old-fashioned or electric. Remember the history of cauldrons and the need for humanity to boil water for cleaning, cooking, and purifying? Many cultures throughout the world have developed elaborate rituals involving tea and coffee, which is a way of celebrating this early achievement. And if the popularity of cafes and tea shops is any indication, we're still celebrating that connection and renewing its ritual in new ways for the modern era. (Think about *that* the next time you're at Starbucks.)

So how do we become more conscientious about our own practices and look at them from a magical perspective? Let's start with the kettle and look at the process of distribution. The kettle's primary purpose is to heat the water. From there, the water is poured into a loaded teapot to be brewed into tea and then dispersed into cups; or into a prepared filter that drips into a pot, press, or cup; or directly into a lone cup that's been loaded with a waiting tea bag. (Technically a coffeemaker combines the kettle, filter, and pot process into one.) So we have the heating of the water, the brewing process, and the distribution—three points of ritual contact.

1) As we fill the kettle and heat the water, we can bestow blessings upon the kettle and consider the transforma-

tional process the water will undergo to be purified and prepared for our brew.

2) There is the process of the preparation of the dry part of the brew—whether it be tea leaves, herbs, or coffee grounds—and the marrying of it with the hot water. What components make up the drink? What are their properties and benefits? What are we thinking about as the tea brews inside the teapot or filters through the coffee grounds?

3) Finally, when the brew is ready to be consumed, we can bless the cup that contains it and take that brew into our bodies to nourish us. And if we brew enough for more than just ourselves, we partake in a communal experience, connecting all who share.

Perhaps that's a bit more in depth than you care to be thinking about the office coffeemaker, but it sure does shine a new perspective on things, doesn't it? It may excite you to think more about the kind of blend you're drinking, or make you want to make your own and consider how to coordinate herbs and tea blends to work magick through them. I have included some wonderful tea vendors in the resource section for those of you who love tea, but maybe making your own blends isn't how you want to spend your time.

Lastly, you could also bless your favorite kettle, mug, or teacup as your own personal cauldron of wakefulness, elaborating on the sample blessings I included back in chapter 4.

Kettle Blessing

I call upon Ceridwen to bless this kettle. May the water be of perfect temperature, may I always hear the kettle when it's ready, and may the water it boils be pure and inspiring and brew a wondrous cup! In her name, so shall it be.

Teapot Blessing

I call upon the elements to bless this teapot! May fire keep it warm, may water provide a balanced brew, may the herbs be worthy of the earth, and may the air infuse it with the aroma of inspiration. So mote it be.

Mug Blessing

May this mug be the receptacle of all that is good. May it bring me mindfulness, good health, and satisfaction. May it be a sturdy vessel of perfect temperature and refrain from unfortunate spillage. So mote it be.

Crock-Pot and Kitchen Witchery

And then the gods invented the Crock-Pot and all was good. Actually, the inventor of what came to be known as the Crock-Pot was Irving Naxon, an American Jew of Lithuanian descent who was awarded a patent in 1940 for his design of a portable, even-cooking device. He later sold his design to Rival Manufacturing in the 1970s, which in turn gave us the Crock-Pot brand. It is basically a cauldron with its own internal cooking mechanism!

The Crock-Pot is different from a fondue pot or similar kinds of hotpots since they are typically heated by an actual fire or coals—which in turn makes the bottom more hot than the top, causing uneven cooking. Naxon was inspired by a dish his mother made, known as *cholent*—a kind of stew that Jews prepare to help keep the Sabbath—which ritually requires them not to do any work on that holy day, including cooking. The stew goes into a heated stove or cauldron before sundown on Friday and cooks via residual heat until the end of the religious services the next day. I love that the Crock-Pot has a mixture of practical and ritually minded roots!

So what can the Crock-Pot mean to you? The blessing of the design is that you can prepare a meal, place it in the pot, and set it to slowly cook while you do other things. (Be sure to follow the manufacturer's instructions for safely using your Crock-Pot. It can be a potential fire hazard to leave a Crock-Pot unattended.) If you're someone who is intimidated by the practice of kitchen witchery but loves the idea of making magical meals, then the Crock-Pot could be your new best friend. How so? While obscure and more hard-to-obtain herbs certainly hold a lot of allure, there are so many common herbs, spices, and vegetables that you can easily find that also happen to have magical properties! Figure out what kind of magical meal you'd like to make and what ingredients would be best for it, then find a slow-cooker recipe that fits, and you're on your way. You can make meals that bring love, foster understanding, welcome a new member, honor the ancestors, etc.

Let's start by looking at a list of magical meanings of some easily found ingredients that might be part of a Crock-Pot recipe:

Almond: Blessing, bonding

Anise Seed: Love and romance

Apple: Good luck, happiness, fertility

Basil: Courage and strength

Beets: Love and romance

Celery and Celery Seed: Strong mental abilities, insight

Cinnamon: Love, purification

Cloves: Kinship, psychic abilities

Corn: Fertility, blessings

Cumin: Balance, prosperity

Dill: Good fortune, health

Fennel: Long life, protection

Fenugreek: Happiness and cheer

Fig: Courage, wisdom

Garlic: Protection, health

Ginger: Health, good energy

Lemon: Romance, cleansing

Mints: Blessings, clarity

Mushrooms: Fertility, joy

Orange: Safe travel, romance, clear thinking, purification

Parsley: Healing, good fortune

Pepper: Understanding, protection, strengthen relationships

Potato: Life-giving, container of spirit/energy

Rice: Offerings, fertility, forming bonds

Rosemary: Stimulating memory, loyalty, love

Sage: Healing, purification

Sesame Seeds: Protection

Tarragon: Compassion, independence

Thyme: Lightheartedness, confidence

Turmeric: Safe journeys, success

Wheat: Fertility, life

Thinking Outside the Cauldron

Stirring the Cauldron:
Samhain Harvest Soup

I MAKE THIS soup in the fall, especially around Samhain/Halloween, and serve it with crusty bread or in bread bowls as a main dish. It's also good as a side dish and can be extended with the addition of rice for leftovers. It always makes me feel "autumnal," and the use of the root vegetables and gourds, for me, is a connection to the holiday's representation of the final harvest before the cold of winter. I live in a place where the idea of a cold, hard winter is not very common, but being able to connect to the holiday's food traditions using the ingredients (gourd, root vegetables) and make a big batch for my family and friends makes me feel more connected to the traditions behind it. I also make this soup for the night when I set my ancestor altar and leave some out for my grandparents, who did live mostly subsistence lifestyles as children and young adults, and who would have been very in touch with the need to make sure the last harvest before winter was a good one.

Variation A

Ingredients

1 tablespoon butter or oil

½ cup to 1 cup chopped onion

4–5 cups steamed, mashed pumpkin OR (if you want to go the easiest route) 3–4 cans of mashed pumpkin (make sure it's legit pumpkin and not pie filling!)

1 cup mashed carrots or parsnips, steamed to soften or (easy route) buy frozen and heat up and then mash

6 cups broth (chicken or veggie is best)—this amount will vary based on personal preference for a thicker or thinner soup, but 6 cups is about average

12 ounces beer—aim for medium or light, as dark beer will give a bitter aftertaste here; pumpkin ale works well but is not necessary

2–3 large (or equivalent amount of smaller) potatoes, raw—this comes out to about 1½ pounds, in my experience

8 ounces cream (dairy or vegetarian version) at room temperature

Tarragon to taste—I usually end up using about 1 tablespoon fresh or 1 teaspoon dried for a 3-quart pot

Directions

Set Crock-Pot on high to melt butter/heat oil. When it has melted/heated, turn the temperature down to medium setting to prevent burning. If your pot only has "keep warm," "low," and "high," set it to "low."

Add the onion. Let it simmer while you mash together the pumpkin and carrots/parsnips. Mash as smooth as possible! Add to Crock-Pot and slowly pour in liquids except cream.

Add in chopped potatoes and put a lid on the pot. Let cook for 4–6 hours or until potatoes are done. If you need to let it cook longer, adjust the setting to low so as not to overcook the potatoes. Add cream before serving.

Variation B

Substitute 1 can of coconut cream (Thai style, not the kind used for mixed drinks) in place of the beer. Remove the addition of dairy-style cream entirely.

Add curry powder instead of tarragon during the mixing phase—use your favorite curry powder and adjust to taste, but as pumpkin is fairly sweet, add more than you think you need; I usually go for 2 tablespoons plus a dash or two over

Reduce the amount of potatoes by half (can also be removed entirely for a smoother soup here)

Cook on low to prevent scorching or curdling, about 4–5
hours.

Meredith Spies
**Author, performer, and
Kitchen Witch living in
the Southeast •
www.facebook.com/meredithaspies •
www.twitter.com/meredithspies**

The Stove and Oven: The New Hearth

Ovens and stovetops are pretty standard in most modern
homes these days. They have replaced the need to cook your
food in a hearth and tend a fire in order to keep the house warm
(as that's the furnace's job). While a home may have a fireplace (most of them now are decorative models with fake logs
and gas flame), it's often no longer the center of the house—
which the hearth also was. That means the hearth of old has
migrated with the cooking processes to the modern kitchen of
today. Think about it: If you're utilizing your cauldron for cooking indoors, you're getting your heat source from the stovetop
or oven. While many households have a formal dining room,
family members often gather for meals and catch up with each
other in the kitchen. So while they may not house a big fire, the
stove and oven are the hearth of today's home—and can also be
the center of your magical workings!

Thinking Outside the Cauldron

An old-fashioned hearth cauldron

Keeping A Good Working Hearth

If my stove is a mess, it makes me feel like the rest of the kitchen and even the rest of the house is a mess. Inversely, if the stove is clean, everything else seems closer to being in order—which makes sense when you consider the stove to be the central hearth. I find that if I take an extra couple of minutes after I have finished cooking to wipe down the surface of the stove, it's far easier to keep it clean. If you let it build up, it definitely becomes a chore, and meal by meal it becomes a less pleasant place in which to work. You can also have a small altar over or near your stove and oven to help remind you to keep them clean and be in a magical frame of mind. Since cooking grease and smoke can build up, only place things on your stove that you can easily clean by wiping it down or with a good soapy soak.

Tip: I always leave the oven door cracked open in the winter after I'm done using it so that the extra heat can warm up the house—just like the hearth used to.

Deities and Spirits of the Hearth

As you may imagine with cooking and the hearth being core to the development of civilization, there are countless practices and much folklore associated with the hearth. There are deities who have specific domain over the hearth, as well as a variety of household spirits in nearly every culture. A common practice when you're cooking or brewing something is to always put aside a small serving to be offered in thanks to the gods or spirits. (If the concept of household spirits intrigues you, I recommend reading *The Tradition of Household Spirits* by Claude Lecouteux.)

Here are some goddesses of the hearth:

Aspelenie (Slavic): She appears in the form of a small, friendly snake to guard and protect the hearth.

Brigid (Celtic): She is a keeper of the flame and a goddess of poetry, fertility, and blacksmithing.

Frigg (Norse): She is the wife of Odin and a bearer of foresight.

Hestia (Greek): Hestia's name means "hearth," and she oversees the home, family, and domestic balance.

Vesta (Roman): She is the goddess of matters of the hearth, family, and home, and a perpetual fire was kept in her temple.

Hearth Blessing

I call upon Hestia, goddess of the hearth, to bless this stove. May its flame burn safely, may the air be filled with pleasant aromas from its brews, may the food cooked upon it bring good health, and may water keep it clean and pure. May the family of this house and all of its guests find joy, happiness, love, and well-being through the fruits and use of this hearth. So mote it be.

Simmer Pots

One of the most magical things I've learned from my mother is the use of the simmering pot. At certain times of the year, she brings together herbs and spices in a pot of water and lets it slowly brew on the stove at a low temperature. The result of this practice is a wonderful aroma that fills the entire home.

To Brew: Place the ingredients in the pot, and fill two-thirds of the way with water. How much of the ingredients you use depends on the size of your pot. I tend to use a pot that holds at least 2–3 cups of water, and the ingredients just about line the bottom of the pan before I add the water. Less is more, so add as you go.

Note: Even with the heat on low, the water will eventually evaporate, which can cause the pot to scorch and the ingredients to burn. Be sure to check on your pot regularly, and add more water and ingredients as needed. I also use a specific saucepan for this purpose, which is helpful if you *do* forget so you don't accidentally ruin your favorite pan.

Simmer Pot Recipes
Here are some recipes to inspire you.

For a Happy Home
Ingredients: Cloves, nutmeg, cinnamon sticks, orange slices

For Cleansing and Purifying
Ingredients: Lemon slices, marigold petals, St. John's wort, garlic

For Prosperity
Ingredients: Mint, rosemary, lime slices, basil

Thinking Outside the Cauldron

For Peace and Serenity
Ingredients: Vanilla, lavender, lemon slices, anise seed

For Love and Comfort
Ingredients: Rosehips, pomegranate seeds, fig, nutmeg, orange slices

> **Tip:** If you're looking to combine the simmer pot with something you can also drink, look into recipes for mulled wine. It's fairly easy and a great way to make a blessed or sacred wine for a ritual.

Stirring the Cauldron:
Two Cauldron Recipes

HERE ARE TWO cauldron recipes. One is an apple cake my mom always made for Samhain and sometimes for Mabon. The corn bread is another old recipe that has been in my mother's family for generations. It is a great harvest bread and is always the base for our sage stuffing. Both are simple recipes and are tasty.

Apple Cake

4 cups apples, peeled and chopped into ½-inch chunks

3 eggs, beaten

2 cups sugar

1 cup oil (grapeseed oil works great)

2 cups flour, sifted

1 teaspoon salt

1 tablespoon cinnamon

¼ teaspoon nutmeg

1 teaspoon baking soda

1 teaspoon vanilla

Preheat oven to 350°F. Grease the cauldron (large Dutch oven), rubbing butter halfway up the side of the cauldron and on the bottom and then lightly dusting with flour before filling with the batter. In a separate bowl, mix all the ingredients using a wooden spoon, then pour into the cauldron. Bake with the lid off for 1 hour or until a bamboo skewer poked in the center pulls free clean.

Savory Fall Cornbread

$^1/_3$ cup oil (grapeseed oil or bacon grease work well)

1 cup flour

1 cup cornmeal

1 teaspoon salt

$^1/_4$ cup sugar

1 tablespoon baking powder

$^1/_3$ cup onion flakes

$^1/_3$ cup dried parsley

1 cup milk

1 egg

Preheat oven to 400°F. Pour the oil in the cauldron (cast-iron Dutch oven) and warm the oil. Coat the sides of the cauldron with the warm oil. In a separate bowl, mix the dry ingredients, then add the egg, milk, and warmed oil. Mix well but do not over-beat. A wooden spoon works better than an electric mixer (lumps are okay). Pour the batter into the cauldron and bake with the lid off for 25 minutes or until golden brown.

Diana Ewing
A Kitchen Witch in the tradition of her mother and grandmother, Diana blends food and drink with spells for her family, friends, and coven.

The Spiritual Cauldron

We're going to round out this book by exploring the spiritual cauldron—the one you're *not* going to find at an occult shop or antique store. Just as it's important to take care of your physical cauldron to get work done and be successful, it's also vital to consider the wear and tear that your spiritual cauldron can endure. It's hard to do much of anything when you're feeling worn down, depressed, uninspired, or confused about your spiritual path. My hope is that if and when you ever feel that way, you can use this chapter to invigorate, transform, and renew yourself.

The Cauldron of Poesy

Perhaps giving us yet another layer of insight into the symbolism of the cauldron myths, especially those from Celtic lore, is an Irish bardic poem dating from the seventh century. Named "The Cauldron of Poesy" by modern scholars, it was found in a sixteenth-century manuscript and references three "internal" cauldrons found within the human body: the Cauldron of Warming, the Cauldron of Motion, and the Cauldron of Wisdom. (There are multiple translations of the poem—I recommend looking at the work of Erynn Rowan Laurie and Mary Pat Lynch listed in the bibliography for further investigation.) Each cauldron is positioned in a different part of the human body, somewhat reminiscent of the Indian concept of *chakras*—specific energy wheels situated throughout the body that guide its functions and processes.

The Cauldron of Warming is located within the pelvic region, below the navel. It starts in the upright position, containing the basic energy and wisdom we need to live, breathe, and grow. Considering that both our digestive and reproductive systems are located in the area of the Cauldron of Warming, this cauldron symbolizes our most animal, instinctive self and provides what fuels us to live in the most basic and essential ways.

The Cauldron of Motion is located in the center of the chest near the heart and lungs, and the poem indicates that we are born with it on its side. If you think of your cauldron being on its side, that means it contains some energy but isn't in the ideal position to receive or hold more. This cauldron could be succinctly described as "what moves us, makes us." The poem speaks in depth about how the Cauldron of Motion is most influenced by poetry and artistic pursuits, cultural and academic exploration, and allowing ourselves to experience both sorrow and joy in turn.

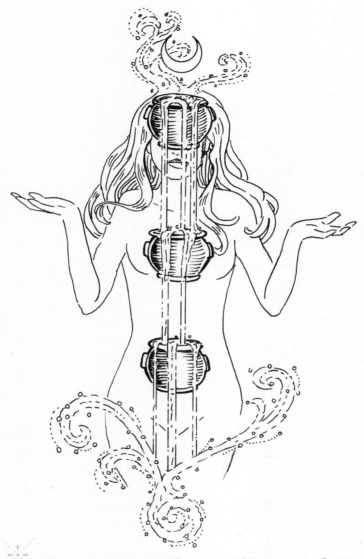

The three cauldrons: the Cauldron of Warming, the Cauldron of Motion, and the Cauldron of Wisdom (from bottom to top)

The Cauldron of Wisdom can be found within or on top of the head, and when we are born, it's resting "on its lips," which means it's upside down—empty! This cauldron rules our spiritual development, helping us to see connections between ourselves, our paths, the gods, and one another. It's related to being aware of one's purpose and making wise choices accordingly.

If we think of all three cauldrons being right-side up and receiving, then they become a flowing fountain of energy, feeding each other and the soul. But that is not an easy task! The positioning of these cauldrons (right-side up, tipped, or overturned), as well as what we may have brewing inside of them, is said to have a lot to do with how inspired we are and the state of our emotional, physical, mental, and spiritual well-being. This is certainly a very interesting way to envision the connection between physical, inspirational, and emotional health. I also think it may be easier for some folks to visualize and connect with these three cauldrons than with some other systems. It certainly gives new meaning to the phrase "to upset someone's cauldron."

If you're not of an artistic persuasion, it may be difficult for you to relate to poetry and inspiration as fuel for living, but I invite you to think of it as a way of seeing the beauty of the world and finding out what makes you tick. For some people that's all about making art or music, while for others it's teaching middle school, practicing defense law, engineering, or programming. What moves you is what inspires you.

The Cauldron Born

I've heard this phrase applied in a variety of different contexts:

- Describing the soldiers who were brought back to life via the cauldron
- Heroes whose lives were drastically changed by an interaction with a cauldron
- All of us, in the framework of "The Cauldron of Poesy," as we are all born with cauldrons
- As a way to describe those who are "of the Craft"

I would like to offer another perspective to the mix: all of us who have been affected by the Cauldron of Change. I see the Cauldron of Change as a crucible, a purifier, a maker, and a transformer. It can be anything in our lives that sets us on a new path or gives us a new perspective—and in turn invigorates and inspires us. It can happen through divorce, a job loss, a health crisis, social change—pretty much anything signified by the Tower card of the Tarot. Everything gets upended, yet we are able to find our feet and a new direction.

Not only can the Cauldron of Change affect us personally, but it can also be a tool to bring about greater social awareness, equality, and balance. It seeks to hold a scrying mirror up to society, to shift our perception, clarifying our vision in order to make us see, feel, and connect deeper. It happens one person at a time, just like the way that water comes to a boil—individual particles slowly moving, until the whole thing is rolling and rumbling. That's how change comes about.

I offer to you this chant to use for spellcraft or meditation to help inspire and bring change where you see it needed.

> *Cauldron of Change, vessel of might,*
> *Within your walls, we gain new sight.*
> *Stirred and whirled, bubble and brew,*
> *Moving all we thought we knew.*
> *Shaken far from the fallen tower,*
> *Birthed and born within your power.*
> *New life, new heart, and new eyes,*
> *To breathe again under better skies.*

Trance Meditation

Trance meditation and similar forms of visualization can be extremely empowering. These techniques can be used for divination and revelation, or they can be an initiatory experience and give you a first-person look inside a myth or legend. I've also used trance meditation for relaxation, spellcraft, and healing work.

I learned trance meditation from one of my dear mentors, Robert Mathiesen. In college, I was lucky enough to work with him in an independent study course, and we spent a fair bit of time doing trance meditation. Even though it's been nearly twenty years, I still vividly remember the work we did together and it has greatly influenced how I modeled much of my own trance practices. When leading a trance exploration, he often combines several fantastic traditional myths to create a new kind of "meta-myth"—reminding me that myth is always growing and changing with our experience.

The main method of trance meditation that I learned from Robert involves taking three deep, slow breaths and concentrating on the energy in your body as a pool or cloud. Then step by step, the pool recedes (or the cloud shrinks), pulling in toward your solar plexus. At step one, you feel the energy flowing out all the way to your fingers and toes, and move it into your palms and feet. Then from there you move it to your wrists and ankles, elbows and knees, and so forth until you have collected all of the pool of energy into your torso, except for your head. In your head, you consciously turn off the senses you don't need for the meditation, and tell the voices to be quiet, and drain the energy down your neck to the center. Then you draw all of the energy gathered in your torso into a ball and allow it to slowly start turning on itself. Then you count down from ten to one, keeping yourself calm and relaxed, imagining yourself in a safe place, and then begin the journey. This place is one of your own devising; it can be a room, a house, a grove, a cave, a ship—whatever makes you feel safe and protected as you enter liminal space. I typically imagine a sunny one-room cottage that has a door I can go through to begin the journey.

When you're done, come back to your safe place, count backward from ten, and visualize yourself as that ball of energy. Slow the ball down, make it still, and start to disperse it in reverse. Return the energy and senses back to your head and then in flowing waves through the rest of your body. Once you've come back fully to yourself, write down what you thought, felt, and saw.

Tip: Trance meditation is a wonderful exercise to lead with a group of people, or if you have only you at your disposal, record yourself counting down the steps and then speaking the meditation. Give yourself time and don't rush.

The Inner Cauldrons Meditation

I wrote this meditation to help you further explore the Cauldron of Poesy concept. It begins once you have arrived in your safe place.

When you are ready, open the door and head outside, where it is a beautiful day. As you look around, you see beautiful rolling green hills and gorgeous blue skies sprinkled with clouds.

The air is fresh and the birds are singing. You spy in the distance, perhaps about half a mile away, what looks to be a small hill with standing stones on it. Before you is a small worn dirt path through the grass heading to the hill. With a spring in your step, you head down the path, following the sun and passing small herds of sheep. As the sheep graze, you hear the bells around their necks chime softly, occasionally interspersed with bleets and baas as they raise their heads to look at you and then return to eating their breakfast.

As the sun rises higher, you draw closer to the hill, and you notice that the standing stones are much larger than you thought they were. There are three large ones in particular that seem like solemn, peaceful giants watching the world. You finally reach the base of the hill and follow the path around the back, where you find a cairn of sorts with an opening. There are two stones the size of a person on either side of the entrance, plus one more balanced on top of them set into the hill, and then seven stone steps leading down to somewhere. It's so bright out that it's hard to see what's down there, but it doesn't feel scary or threatening, so you go down the stairs, into the cool earth.

Once inside, your eyes adjust to the space, where there are three gleaming metal cauldrons standing on pillars in the center of the space, illuminated by lanterns—and their guardian. The guardian is a person of considerable age with long gray hair, and you're not quite sure if you're looking at a man or a woman, but their eyes are kind and they seem familiar to you. They greet you with a smile but do not speak. Instead they gesture to the cauldron on the far left and nod for you to go to it. You stand in front of it and see that it reads "The Cauldron of Warming." The guardian indicates for you to put your hands on the cauldron.

You take a breath and reach out, touching your hands to the smooth metal, which is surprisingly warm. You close your eyes and start to feel as if you are touching your own belly, but your hands are still on the cauldron. A voice says to you, "This is the Cauldron of Warming. It is what incubated you as a child and set you on your path. It is the basis for your physical health and well-being. You were born with it full and upright, but how is it situated now? What color is it to you? Does it feel upright, tipped, or upside down? Is it losing or gaining content? Breathe and examine your cauldron." (Allow for 2–3 minutes of contemplation.)

Next you hear the voice say, "Open your eyes and embrace the cauldron to your right, the Cauldron of Motion." You follow the instructions and place your hands on this cauldron. This one feels cooler to your touch and has many patterns etched on its surface. You close your eyes and find yourself feeling as if your hands are resting against your chest instead of the cauldron. The voice says, "The Cauldron of Motion is your state of being in the world. It's what drives you to make, to move, to build, to grow, to laugh, and to cry. Through it, you experience all of the sorrows and joys this world has to offer. It was born tipped in you, but how does it sit now? What color is it to you? Does it feel upright, tipped, or upside down? Is it losing or gaining content? Breathe and examine your cauldron." (Allow for 2–3 minutes of contemplation.)

The voice speaks again: "Open your eyes and embrace the final cauldron, the Cauldron of Wisdom." You follow the instructions and place your hands on the last cauldron. This one has a slight vibration to it, a sense of humming or chiming. You close your eyes and find yourself feeling as if your hands are placed upon your head instead of the cauldron. The voice says, "The Cauldron of Wisdom is your spiritual connection to all things, from yourself to the divine. When you were born, it was upside down, but how is it situated now? What color is it to you? Does it feel upright, tipped, or upside down? Is it losing or gaining content? Breathe and examine your cauldron." (Allow for 2–3 minutes of contemplation.)

You realize that the humming of the cauldron has stopped and you feel a soft breeze on your face. You open your eyes and find yourself not in a dark room with three cauldrons but standing in front of the hill with the standing stones. You walk the path around the hill, but there is no cairn, no opening, no guardian. You notice that the sun has journeyed quite a distance while you were in the cave, so you follow the path back home, watching the sun slowly sink in the sky, filling it with soft yellow, rose, and purple tones. The sheep come along with you as you pass them, bleeting merrily the whole way, with their bells ringing, until you reach the door of the cottage. You turn around, taking one last look back at where you just came from, seeing the silhouette of the stones far off. You smile and turn toward the door, entering your safe place once again. Take a moment to think about each of your cauldron experiences. What did you see? What did you feel? What did you learn? Hold on to these, and prepare yourself to return to your body.

The Ultimate Cauldron

Lastly, in examining the many facets of the spiritual cauldron, I would like to introduce you to the ultimate cauldron that you already are in possession of: your body. Imagine your physical body as the vessel that contains the essence of you within its walls. Your body can also be used to temporarily house spirits and gods, through ritual and trance states. I would say that one of the most amazing parts of being human is experiencing and interacting with the physical world as a spirit housed in a vessel of flesh and bone.

Like anything you might brew in your cast-iron cauldron, there is an integral relationship between your spirit and your body. If you apply too much heat to your brew for too long, it can evaporate or scorch. If you leave something acidic or waxy in your cauldron, it can affect how well it functions later on. Metaphorically, the same is true for your spirit and body. If you are too hard on your body, it can drastically affect your health and, in turn, your overall well-being. Inversely, there are numerous ills of the spirit that can impact your body. It's easy to get caught up in the grind of daily life without taking the time to rest your body properly. You can also give endlessly to others who don't reciprocate, draining you of your essence and wearing you down mentally and spiritually.

To care for your ultimate cauldron, it's important to take time to eat properly, get enough sleep, hydrate, and take time to rest as well as play. Set aside a few moments each day to connect with yourself—from considering your daily and yearly goals to checking in with your spiritual health. This may all seem like common sense, but unfortunately in this day and age, we're often obsessed with all of the things we feel we *have* to do and forget to make time for the things we *need* to do (present company included).

Much of what was covered in chapter 8 is ideal for fostering a self-care schedule that will stimulate your senses, body, and mind. You can use kitchen witchery to cook meals that not only are good for the body but can be shared with family and friends. Remember those feasting cauldrons? They bring everyone together in addition to providing nourishment—a feast for the soul! Brewing your own beverages, from mulled wine to a lovely cup of tea, does a world of good for both the body and the mind, especially when you introduce a nuance of ritual to it. Bathtime not only cleans the body but also relaxes it and cleanses the spirit.

There's also the matter of dressing and decorating the body to affect the mind. Billy Crystal on *Saturday Night Live* had a skit called "Fernando's Hideaway" (based on the actor Fernando Lamas), where his catchphrase was "You look marvelous!" In one particular episode that I will always remember, he said, "If you look marvelous, you will *feel* marvelous!"—one of the best arguments for glamour magick I can think of! We've become a very casual society, which is great in some regards and sad in others. Dressing up, even if it's just to go run errands, can provide a confidence boost. Getting a haircut or trying a different style, doing your nails, playing with make-up—all are very simple ways to affect your physical container while helping to adjust your spirit a bit! Sometimes it's very hard to be kind to ourselves, as society tends to put a lot of pressure on us and have strong opinions about how we should look. The best thing you can do is to make choices that feel right for you and help boost your confidence in your day-to-day life, without being down on yourself or others. Confidence is a bit like cat hair—start with a little, and soon you'll be covered in it! Be gentle with yourself, be adventurous enough to take on a new perspective, and most of all, have some fun!

The Confident Cauldron Mantra

My feet are on the earth, my walls are strong and round.
Within me brews a mighty spirit, beautiful and sound!

In Conclusion: Putting the Lid on the Cauldron

Thank you so much for traveling with me on this cauldron journey. I hope that you have found this book to be informative and enlightening, adding new dimensions and insight to your personal practice. Whether you purchase, find, or make your cauldron, may you look at it with new eyes and a deeper sense of connection to its long history and exciting future. Don't be afraid to think outside of the circle, finding new meanings and ways of working. Remember that Witchcraft, at its heart, is an unconventional path! I hope your own cauldron of inspiration has been stirred, empowering you to play, to explore, and to develop your own Craft traditions. Blessed be!

Acknowledgments

I am blessed to have so many wonderful people in my life who are incredibly supportive and inspiring. Much love and appreciation to my family and friends, especially to my mother, Terry Zakroff, who did a whirlwind round of proofreading, and my husband, Nathaniel, who is my cauldron of inspiration. (You wouldn't believe how hard it is to refer to your partner and make a cauldron reference without it getting...nuanced. *Ahem.*)

Much gratitude to Paul Beyerl and the Rowan Tree Church for granting me access to their amazing library on herbal lore, letting me pick Paul's incredibly knowledgeable brain, and giving me a tour of their beautiful grounds in Kirkland,

Washington. Please check out www.therowantreechurch.org and www.thehermitsgrove.org for more information on their events, services, garden tours, resources, and herbalism classes and programs.

Big thanks to Jake von Slatt for his technical input and expertise on metal interactions and their related dangers. Thanks to Shakira for supporting my tiny cauldron habit. Thank you to Erynn Rowan Laurie for helping me out when I found out about yet another cauldron reference. My ongoing appreciation to Robert Mathiesen for his insight, guidance, and support over the years. Big Pikachu hugs to Elysia Gallo for believing I could do this thing. Thanks to all the P-words who bore witness to my online posts/rants and silly comments as I worked my way through this project—and for supporting my work in all its forms!

Last but not least, a big cauldron full of thanks to all of the "Stirring the Cauldron" conspirators/contributors for lending their voices and experiences to this project—you rock!

Bibliography

Ancient History Encyclopedia. www.ancient.eu.

Bellows, Henry Adams, trans. *The Poetic Edda: Hymiskviða.* 1936. www.sacred-texts.com/neu/poe/poe09.htm.

Beyerl, Paul. *A Compendium of Herbal Magick.* Custer, WA: Phoenix Publishing, 1998.

———. *The Master Book of Herbalism.* Custer, WA: Phoenix Publishing, 1984.

British Museum. www.britishmuseum.org and blog.britishmuseum.org.

Broad, William J. *The Oracle: Ancient Delphi and the Science Behind Its Lost Secrets.* New York: Penguin, 2006.

Bromwich, Rachel, ed. and trans. *Tri Thlws ar Ddeg.* Cardiff: University of Wales Press, 1978.

Cascone, Sarah. "Gold Cauldron Found in Lake Attributed to Nazi Goldsmith Otto Gahr Sparks Lawsuit." ArtNetNews. March 6, 2015. https://news.artnet.com/market/ancient -gold-cauldron-lawsuit-274597.

Cunningham, Scott. *Cunningham's Encyclopedia of Crystal, Gem & Metal Magic.* Woodbury, MN: Llewellyn, 2002.

———. *Cunningham's Encyclopedia of Magical Herbs.* St. Paul, MN: Llewellyn, 1999.

Ewbank, Thomas. *A Descriptive and Historical Account of Hydraulic and Other Machines for Raising Water, Ancient and Modern; Including the Progressive Development of the Steam Engine.* London: Tilt and Bogue, 1842.

Farrar, Janet and Stewart. *The Witches' God.* Custer, WA: Phoenix Publishing, 1989.

———. *The Witches' Goddess.* Custer, WA: Phoenix Publishing, 1987.

Fries, Jan. *Cauldron of the Gods: A Manual of Celtic Magick.* Oxford, UK: Mandrake of Oxford, 2003.

Gantz, Jeffrey, trans. *The Mabinogion.* New York: Penguin, 1987.

Guest, Lady Charlotte E., intro. and trans. *The Mabinogion.* Mineola, NY: Dover Publications, 1997.

Homer. *The Odyssey.* Translated by Samuel Butler. http:// classics.mit.edu/Homer/odyssey.html.

Johnston, Sarah Iles. *Ancient Greek Divination.* Chichester, West Sussex: John Wiley & Sons, 2009.

Laurie, Erynn Rowan. "The Cauldron of Poesy." Article provided to the author. For more information, see www.seanet.com/~inisglas/cauldronpoesy.html.

———. *Ogam: Weaving Word Wisdom.* Stafford, UK: Megalithica Books, 2007.

Lecouteux, Claude. *The Tradition of Household Spirits: Ancestral Lore and Practices.* Rochester, VT: Inner Traditions, 2013.

Lynch, Mary Pat, PhD. "The Three Cauldrons of Poesy: Dreams, Visions and Ancestry." Lecture, IASD Conference, Montreal, 2008. http://threecauldrons.com /writing/written/ThreeCauldronsMontreal08MPL.pdf.

National Museum of Denmark. en.natmus.dk.

Ristic, Radomir. *Balkan Traditional Witchcraft.* Los Angeles, CA: Pendraig Publishing, 2009.

Stoneman, Richard. *The Ancient Oracles: Making the Gods Speak.* New Haven, CT: Yale University Press, 2011.

Sturluson, Snorri. *The Prose Edda: Gylfaginning.* Translated by Arthur Gilchrist Brodeur. 1916. www.sacred-texts.com /neu/pre/pre04.htm.

Valiente, Doreen. *Witchcraft for Tomorrow.* Custer, WA: Phoenix Publishing, 1978.

Credits for "A Heathen's Cauldron" By Sarah Bennett:

Gundarsson, Kveldúlfr. *Things, Signs, and Their Meanings: A Dictionary of Heathen Symbols.* New Haven, CT: The Troth, 2010.

Sarah Bennett's Suggested Links for Further Reading:

"Alcoholic Beverages and Drinking Customs of the Viking Age." The Viking Answer Lady. www.vikinganswerlady.com/drink.shtml.

Andersen, Mark. "Beer and Brewing Culture Through the Eyes of a New England Heathen." Odroerir: The Heathen Journal. April 2012. http://odroerirjournal.com/beer-and-brewing-culture-through-the-eyes-of-a-new-england-heathen.

Recommended Reading & Resources

In addition to the source material in the bibliography, I highly recommend checking out the following books and publications.

Drawing Down the Moon by Margot Adler

If you're interested in learning more about modern Paganism, this is the number-one book I recommend for getting an overall look at the history of Neopaganism and many of the branches you will find. Alas, Margot passed away in 2014, so we won't get any further updates from her, but I hope someone will carry the torch and keep track of cultural developments for a future edition.

Natural Magic, The Rebirth of Witchcraft, **and** *Witchcraft for Tomorrow* **by Doreen Valiente**

Next up on my list are these three books by Valiente, known to be the mother of modern Witchcraft/Wicca. Much of the beautiful poetic language that you can find in Wicca came from Doreen—and she continued to research historical Witchcraft and folklore after parting ways with Gerald Gardner. I love her attitude and her no-nonsense approach, seasoned with a dash of whimsy.

The Triumph of the Moon **by Ronald Hutton**

This is a good book to add to the shelf. A professor of history at the University of Bristol, Hutton provides a lot of in-depth research concerning the history of modern Paganism. This book caused quite an uproar when it came out in 1999, and has made fascinating waves of impact on the culture since then.

If you're looking for information on a specific culture, the best place to look *first* is in the folklore/anthropology section of your local bookstore or library. Folklore and myth can really inform us about the practices and beliefs of old, directly from the source. The more you read about the stories from a culture, the better you can understand it.

With the rising cost of print media, there are fewer hard-copy Pagan magazines on the market, but a subscription to *Witches & Pagans* magazine from BBI Media will definitely make you and your mailbox happy. You can also enjoy their online blogosphere at http://witchesandpagans.com. If you're into reading blogs, check out the wealth of Pagan voices you can feast your eyes and brain on at www.patheos.com/Pagan.

Following the Author Online

I write several weekly and monthly blogs, where I write about witchy things:

A Modern Traditional Witch: www.patheos.com/blogs/tempest

Fine Art Witchery: http://witchesandpagans.com/pagan
-paths-blogs/fine-art-witchery

The Modern Tradition of Witchcraft: www.moderntraditional
witch.com

Regarding Herbs and Magick

As I've mentioned several times in the book, it's important to understand the herbs you're using. The books I listed by Paul Beyerl and Scott Cunningham in the bibliography are must-haves if you're interested in using herbs in any way. If you're interested in learning more about "baneful" herbs (those of the poisonous variety), I recommend also acquiring *How Do Witches Fly? A Practical Approach to Nocturnal Flights* by Alexander Kuklin, *Pharmako/Poeia: Plant Powers, Poisons, and Herbcraft* by Dale Pendell, and *The Witches' Ointment: The Secret History of Psychedelic Magic* by Thomas Hatsis. Sarah Anne Lawless's blog at http://sarahannelawless.com is another good resource to get you started.

Incenses, Teas, and More

Here are some recommended artisans:

Artemisia Botanicals: www.artemisiabotanicals.com— Huge selection of herbs, oils, and other supplies.

B. Fuller's Mortar & Pestle (Artisanal Modern Apothecary): www.bfullers.com—Classic, herbal, and botanical teas, bath blends, and accessories.

Bastet's Bath: www.bastetsbath.com—Handcrafted bath bombs with a witchy flair.

Dryad Tea: http://dryadtea.com—Loose-leaf tea blends with creative inspirations.

Rosarium Blends: http://rosariumblends.com—An array of incense, perfume, essential oil blends, and accessories.

Rare Earth Designs: www.rareearthdesigns.net—They not only make beautiful sacred objects out of wood (such as wands), but they also collect and sell the shavings made in the creation of those pieces in an extensive variety of woods—perfect for small fires and other workings.

To Write to the Author

If you wish to contact the author or would like more information about this book, please write to the author in care of Llewellyn Worldwide and we will forward your request. Both the author and the publisher appreciate hearing from you and learning of your enjoyment of this book and how it has helped you. Llewellyn Worldwide cannot guarantee that every letter written to the author can be answered, but all will be forwarded. Please write to:

Laura Tempest Zakroff
Llewellyn Worldwide
2143 Wooddale Drive
Woodbury, MN 55125-2989

Please enclose a self-addressed stamped envelope for reply or $1.00 to cover costs. If outside the USA, enclose an international postal reply coupon.

Many of Llewellyn's authors have websites with additional information and resources. For more information, please visit our website:

WWW.LLEWELLYN.COM